REDISCOVERING OUR SPIRITUAL GIFTS

A Workbook

JOHN I. PENN   *Based on the book by Charles V. Bryant*

UPPER ROOM BOOKS
NASHVILLE

Rediscovering Our Spiritual Gifts: A Workbook

Scripture quotations not otherwise identifed are from the *Holy Bible, New International Version.* Copyright © 1973, 1978, 1984 International Bible Society. Used by permission of Zondervan Bible Publishers.

Scripture quotations designated NRSV are from the New Revised Standard Version of the Bible, © 1989 by the Division of Christian Education of the National Council of the Churches of Christ in the U.S.A. Used by permission. All rights reserved.

Scripture quotations designated RSV are from the Revised Standard Version of the Bible, copyrighted 1946, 1952, and © 1971 by the Division of Christian Education, National Council of the Churches of Christ in the United States of America. Used by permission.

The Upper Room Web Site : http://www.upperroom.org

Cover Design: Cindy Helms
Interior Design: Charles Sutherland
First Printing: June 1996 (5)
Second Printing: September 1997 (3)

Library of Congress Cataloging-in-Publication Data

Penn, John I. , 1939–
      Rediscovering our spiritual gifts : a workbook / John I. Penn.
          p.   cm .
      "Companion resource to Charles Bryant's Rediscovering our
spiritual gifts"—Introd.
      ISBN 0-8358-0771-1
      1. Gifts, Spiritual.   I. Bryant , Charles V. , 1930. Rediscovering
our spiritual gifts. II. Title.
   BT767.3.P46 1996
   234' .13—dc20   96-11012
                                                                  CIP

Printed in the United States of America

CONTENTS

PREFACE

In *Rediscovering Our Spiritual Gifts*, Charles Bryant lists five religious resources: Worship, The Bible, Prayer, Witnessing, and Power. He believes that these and other religious resources are transformed through the presence and operation of the *charismata*, or grace-gifts. These five religious resources will serve as valuable instruments in this workbook format in the following ways: (1) to engage interaction with the main text and marginal material, (2) to promote group dialogue, (3) to challenge biblical-theological reflection, (4) to use discernment to discover God's will, and (5) to encourage spiritual growth. My walk with the Lord has called me to a new and deeper understandings of the *charismata*, and I am thankful to Dr. Bryant for his insights.

This workbook will help readers to interact with Dr. Bryant's book. The activities challenge individuals to use the opportunities God offers to each of us to use our gifts for the growth and health of the body of Christ, not to simply acquire more information about the gifts.

My hope is that the persons using this workbook will approach this study of the gifts with a sense of purposefulness, joyfulness, and challenge.

John I. Penn

SYMBOLS OF GIFTS

The twelve types of activities of the Holy Spirit are the following:

Worship—Explore creatively new ways to promote authentic worship through the presence and operation of all the gifts, or *charismata*, not just those operated by worship leaders.

The Bible—Used as the divine authority by those persons who desire to be scriptural in their understanding of God's grace and their special grace-gifts.

Prayer— A response to God's will and call upon our lives. We will consider prayer as a means to bring our wills into harmony with God's will. From this perspective, prayer gives birth to ministry as well as sustains it.

Witnessing—To understand the charismatic nature of Christian witness to our shared life in Jesus Christ. When we serve others in Christian love, Christ's presence and power are made visible.

Power—To stress the importance and benefits of the ministry of the priesthood of all believers. To understand that the gifts of believers are powers mighty enough to counteract and dispel the evil powers that threaten to destroy the good in the world.

Operational Signs

The operational signs listed below are used in this study:

New Insight—Each participant is challenged to note the new understanding he or she has gained. Sharing this knowledge with others will strengthen and build up the body of Christ.

Incomplete Data—This activity challenges individuals to gain a biblical and theological understanding of the importance and operation of the gifts. If Christians are to grow and mature, wrong thinking and behaviors must be changed, corrected, or reinforced in positive ways.

Written Reflection—This section includes one or more activities or suggestions for reflection. Write the reflection in the space provided.

Looking Ahead—In each session persons are asked to complete some activity before the next gathering.

Discussion Starter— In some cases more discussion starters than you can use are provided for a session. Use what meets the needs of your group or situation.

Group Sharing—These are activities that go beyond discussion. These may involve a subgroup or the whole group.

Is It I, Lord?—God's calling in Isaiah 6 prompted Isaiah to respond, "Here am I, send me." God is still calling persons to respond to ministry. Individuals will be asked to discern how God is calling them to use their grace-gifts for the growth and health of the body of Christ. This is an ongoing process in the life of believers.

INTRODUCTION

This workbook is designed to be a companion resource to Charles Bryant's *Rediscovering Our Spiritual Gifts* and, as such, is to be used along with that book. Therefore, before reading the workbook session, read the corresponding chapter in Bryant's book.

This workbook will also serve as a leader's guide for group study. I envision this companion resource being used as

- ❦ a special growth experience for the individual or a group;
- ❦ a special seasonal emphasis, such as Pentecost;
- ❦ a means of establishing intimate groups within the life of a local church;
- ❦ a way of helping people discover their grace-gifts as a sense of call and ministry;
- ❦ an experience of renewal for existing groups or the whole local church.

People of all churches are becoming more aware of and more interested in knowing how the *charismata* relate to their own spiritual formation and ministry. This workbook will challenge and motivate those persons who desire to understand the gifts from God's perspective for the edification and building up of the church of Jesus Christ.

Study Approaches

This workbook may be used in several ways: as a six-week individual or group study, as a two- or three-day retreat, or as a five-hour, one-day workshop. The readers will use the workbook while practicing all of the spiritual disciplines: prayer, meditation on scripture, corporate worship, communion with God, reflection, and journaling.

Individual Use

If you enjoy working at your own pace, use the two books in individual study. Use the workbook to meet your needs. You have the freedom to grow at your own pace. You are not bound to a six-week schedule. No matter how you decide to use this workbook, be faithful as you seek to reach your personal goal in discovering your grace-gifts.

The size of the group may vary according to the ability and experience of the leadership.

If this is to be a home group, four to eight persons is a good group size, not including the leaders.

The group should not exceed twelve to fifteen persons.

The time spent together should be focused and noncompetitive.

Select a meeting place that is accessible to all persons, including those with handicapping conditions.

Group Use

If this book is to be used as part of a group study, the group should come to consensus on how to approach the material. Before beginning, agree on a day the group will meet, where, and for how long. Work out the details of any changes. All decisions should be for the good of the entire group. A good rule is not to schedule the study session time to last beyond an hour and a half.

If the group decides to have refreshments, do so at the end of the study time. Keep it simple! Everyone should mutually share in the expense of the refreshments. Support and encourage all of the participants in the group. Allow each member the freedom to participate in the manner that is most comfortable to him or her. Let agape love be the motivating principle of the group.

One advantage of journeying with a group is the built-in support. In addition to that support, group participants experience the rich diversity of gifts and discovery. You will discover other benefits during the group process.

Support each person who shares, and encourage all participants to listen openly and receptively and to show discretion. Remember the presence of the Holy Spirit! Allow the Spirit freedom to work, bringing out the best in each person.

Leaders

Two persons, who work well together, should form the leadership team. Spend time praying together and getting to know each other before the study. Time for prayer and preparation should take place at least three months before the first session.

Seek God's guidance to determine what your responsibilities will be, and put your plans and responsibilities in writing. Both leaders should keep a copy of this list. Keep good records of all changes and strategies. Use the consensus method for making decisions. Encourage and uphold one another. Think of the other person more highly than yourself!

If after the leadership team has been formed and you discover that it will not work out, decide as soon as possible to form a new team. Resolve the problem in Christian love and treat each other with respect and dignity. Depart in the peace of Christ.

The first session is usually the most challenging. Be encouraged; things will certainly get better as the group forms and responds to the material. Remember that you are not alone. Jesus Christ promised to be with each person in ministry. The Holy Spirit is present to comfort, strengthen, encourage, and assist. Be receptive to the Spirit and to each person. Do everything for the glory of God. God's presence and power are available to you.

Pay special attention to Session Six. This session is an extensive session, and a group can not realistically cover all the material in one setting. Therefore, you may choose to divide this session into two or three meetings, depending on the needs of the group. Here are some suggestions as to how you might handle Session Six.

(1) Divide the session into three meetings: This would be the best choice if you want to spend extensive time discussing each gift. This would also be helpful if your group consists of persons who are unfamiliar with the spiritual gifts.

(2) Divide the session into two meetings. If your group is familiar with the spiritual gifts and how they operate, you may choose this option. The first meeting would consist of an overview of the gifts, allowing members to raise any questions or concerns about a particular gift or gifts. The second session would consist of the members identifying and discussing their particular gifts, using the questions in the session as a guide.

Leaders should keep the following suggestions in mind:
1. Read the text and the workbook carefully and plan the sessions. (Read the marginal notes first since they are to guide you through the sessions.)
2. Model openness, integrity, and warmth. A leader should not ask others to share what he or she would not express. Leaders should be the first to share personal experiences.
3. Keep all discussions open and lively. Remember to incorporate humor, especially when sessions seem to be too intense. Remind the group that God gives us the gift of joy and laughter.
4. Encourage reluctant participants to contribute to the discussions; seek ways to prevent an individual from dominating the conversation.
5. Keep the group focused on experiences rather than academic debates.
6. Exercise stewardship of time.
7. Set up the meeting room to be attractive and functional before people gather. Arrange the seating so that it will be comfortable. Make sure that all necessary materials are available.
8. Make sure that all materials are on hand five working days before the first session. Those materials include name tags, copies of the two books, index cards, paper, newsprint, markers, and pencils.
9. Bring your own unique style to the group and use your own words in presentations. Use biblical and contemporary stories to keep sessions fresh and interesting.
10. Feel free to adapt the suggestions to meet the needs of your group. Although one person can lead a group, having two leaders connects different gifts in ministry for the good of all participants.

We are not looking for perfect leaders, but persons who are committed to Christ and who desire to see the body of Christ become everything that God is calling it to be.

Personal Reflection and Recording

The workbook format provides space for writing your thoughts, reflections, and meditations as well as answers to questions. Always approach this section with honesty and integrity. What you get out of the study depends largely on your faithfulness and steadfastness. If there is not sufficient space for recording, write answers in the marginal section.

SESSION ONE

The Meaning and Scope of Spiritual Gifts

Holy Spirit, enlighten my mind and my thinking so that I may get the most out of this study. Help me to remove those barriers or obstacles that might hinder me from receiving all that you desire for me in this study. Guide me to discover my gifts and how to use them for the health and growth of the body of Christ, the church. Amen.

> *You lack no single gift while you wait expectantly for our Lord Jesus Christ to be revealed. God will keep you firm to the end, without reproach on the day of our Lord Jesus Christ. God, alone, calls you to share in the life of Jesus Christ our Lord; and God is faithful (1 Corinthians 1:7-9, Bryant's paraphrase).*

Begin the session by completing the "Gifts of the Holy Spirit" questionnaire on page 19. This is not a test, but merely an informative tool to clarify any misconceptions that you might have regarding the gifts. The answers are printed at the bottom of the questionaire, but you will discover explanations of the answers as you work through the sessions.

Prayerfully read the four basic passages of scripture that specifically deal with the gifts (*charismata*): Romans 12:1-8, 1 Corinthians 12:1-31, Ephesians 4:1-16, and 1 Peter 4:10-11.

These passages form a unity of meaning and purpose. The *charismata* only have meaning and purpose when they are used within the context of the church, the body of Christ. God gives the gifts for the health and wholeness of the church. God uses the gifts of each person to edify and build up the church, maintaining health and wholeness. God uses the gifts as evangelistic tools of the church to serve the needs of the world, thus shaping and reshaping it into a world that conforms to God's creative design and purpose.

Have the group pray this prayer together aloud. Open and close each session with prayer. Ask for volunteers to lead these prayers. Pray for the needs of the group. Use the closing prayer time to pray for those who have special needs.

Allow time for the group to briefly discuss the statements and the rationale for the true or false identification.

Ask for volunteers to read aloud each of the four passages. Discuss the implication of each of the passages. Stress that these passages form a unity of meaning and purpose. This may be a good time for you to share briefly how you learned about the Holy Spirit and the gifts. Allow three to five minutes to share their importance in your life and the life of the church.

Remind the participants that the Spirit of God is actively at work in the world and the church, even though that presence may not always be evident or known.

Discuss how the attitude of your congregation toward the gifts may limit the church's effectiveness in witnessing to the power and presence of Christ in the world. This is not to be a griping or blaming session, but a time for healing and moving forward.

The duty of the church is to teach people about the ministry of the Holy Spirit, but many people are suspicious of anyone who claims to have any knowledge of or interest in the Holy Spirit. People are afraid of things they do not fully understand or cannot experience through their physical senses. Dr. Bryant reminds us that the effectiveness of the church is limited when people are ignorant of the role and ministry of the Holy Spirit.

God gives gifts (*charismata*) to accompany the new spiritual life of the believer. Therefore, the responsibility of each Christian is to learn about the gifts of the Holy Spirit. This study will be more challenging for some than for others. If we approach this spiritual journey seeking God's help, we will not be disappointed. God will meet us at the point of our need.

Spiritual gifts are not given only to the spiritual elite. God gives gifts to everyone who turns to God for salvation in Jesus Christ (Heb. 2:4). If you have accepted the salvation of God, you have received gifts to be shared with the body of Christ. You have received spiritual gifts because you are a spiritual person. Gifts do not make us spiritual nor make us feel superior to others. Gifts enable us to share with others the abundant life Jesus came to bring us (John 10:10). Gifts equip us for the task of living in the kingdom of God. This is a part of the good news of the Gospel.

❧ What, if anything, stands out in your mind as an obstacle or barrier to the Holy Spirit's presence, guidance, or power in your life?

❧ What steps have you taken to overcome these obstacles or barriers between you and the Holy Spirit?

The Biblical Meaning and Scope

Four New Testament passages deal specifically with the gifts: Romans 12:1-8; 1 Corinthians 12:1-31; Ephesians 4:1-16; and 1 Peter 4:10-11. The nature and scope of the gifts can be defined as a means of grace. By grace, it is understood that all gifts, or *charismata*, are for service (*diakonia*).

Gifts are given to every believer to serve others in Christ's name. They enable us to effectively serve the people of God in the church and those outside the church. The Greek word for service is *diakonia*, which is service done for others in the spirit and love of Christ.

Gifts have a divine purpose and are not given to us to be used as we wish. They are not our personal property, nor did we acquire them from a human origin, but we acquired our gifts from a spiritual source. Scripture clearly teaches that God gives us grace-gifts for the good of all people. Our gifts empower us to minister to others in Christ's name.

The Source of Gifts

God is the source of all the gifts and places them in the church, the body of Christ. Although we are to yearn for the gifts, God assigns them to each person. God alone knows what the church needs for its health and wholeness. God alone also knows what gifts best fit each one of us in serving the body of Christ.

When we examine what Paul lists in Romans 12, 1 Corinthians 12-14, and Ephesians 4, we find that Paul believed that preaching, teaching, administration, prophecy, evangelism, tongues, and interpretation were the *charismata* most suited for the edification of the church. All gifts are essential and necessary for the health and growth of the church. What gives them their peculiarity and effectiveness is agape love. Without this motivating agape love, the gifts become ineffective and do not communicate God's true nature which is love.

All Christians Included

Everyone who turns to God for salvation has received a grace-gift for serving the church (Heb. 2:4). Along with the gifts comes responsibility to use them for the ministry and mission of the church so that we bring honor to Christ and glorify God.

Gifts are given to every believer at his or her conversion. Being born of the Spirit is a prerequisite for receiving the gifts of the Spirit. Just as we receive common gifts as the results of our physical birth, we also receive special gifts as the results of our spiritual birth. This destroys any argument that suggests only certain persons receive *charismata* or are superior to other persons.

❦ Read John 14-16. What does Jesus say about the role of the Holy Spirit in the life of the believer?

Can Gifts Be Limited

Paul never intended to list all of the *charismata*, for no one can. He mentioned only the gifts that were either neglected or abused by the Corinthian Christians. Paul commended the Corinthian believers for their giftedness, but rebuked them for their ignorance. He acknowledged that they lacked none of the *charismata*, but had limited their use and effectiveness because they favored the more visible or expressive gifts. As a corrective, Paul pointed out that there were other gifts, which had value and importance (1 Cor. 12:22-25). Paul recognized that by rejecting the so-called less spectacular gifts, the Corinthians were bringing disunity to the church. All the gifts have a special function and place within the church. All are nec-

Discuss this statement with the group: The gifts are the evangelistic ministries of the church.

Read aloud 1 Corinthians 12:31. Also read Bryant's explanation concerning this verse on pages 18–19.

Be sensitive to those persons who may feel that they are not worthy to receive gifts or have a theology that the gifts are not for everyone.

Encourage those persons who are now discovering that they have gifts but are under a lot of guilt because they have never used them to help the church's growth and health. Encourage the group to thank God for their gifts and now dedicate their gifts to God's service.

essary. The contemporary church must learn this lesson. We must value all of God's gifts, including all spiritual gifts.

Gifts, Health, Growth

In describing the church as a body made of diverse parts, Paul described the vertical relationship between Christ and the church and described the horizontal relationship between individuals within the church. When the individuals are not properly relating to one another or to Christ (or to both), this jeopardizes the health of the church. Health or unity cannot exist when the gifts are not being used for building up and edifying the church.

Spiritual, Physical, Psychological, and Social Dimensions

Ask each of the participants to recall when the spiritual realm become a reality and to draw a picture or describe how this reality changed their understanding of the kingdom of God and the reality of this world.

Christians by divine design are complete, yet complex beings because we are made in God's image. Being made in God's image suggests that we are more than just a physical being. Since God is Spirit, we are also spiritual beings.

Dr. Bryant reminds us of some historical developments that have influenced people about the spiritual nature of human beings. He notes the following factors: the rapid advances in physical sciences; a world view presumed by Aristotle and harmonized in religious thought by Thomas Aquinas; contributions of behavioral psychology; and contemporary scientific theory. The church has also held a negative view of the spiritual gifts and has had problems in teaching about the nature and purpose of the Holy Spirit in the life of a Christian and the church.

The *charismata* define who we are in Christ. The gifts give us a new dynamic and new orientation as spiritual beings, adding a new dimension to our humanity, including our mental, physical, emotional, and social aspects. The gifts enhance and influence our physical, psychological, and social dimensions. Although the gifts do not change us physiologically or divorce us from the limitations of our humanity, we experience the transcendent power of God's love. As we obediently use the gifts for others, we enhance and elevate our humanity and manifest the grace of God working within us.

God knows every aspect of our psychological and emotional makeup. God knows what makes us tick, the things that bring us joy or sorrow, and what we can and cannot do. Our gifts influence how we act in relation to ourselves and others in the body of Christ.

Close this session by reading Bryant's passage on page 24.

Dr. Bryant states the following: "The gifts are endowments of specialized energy from the Holy Spirit. With this new energy comes renewed motivation and a new self-esteem related to God's will. . . . The gifted person's level of enthusiasm rises to embrace a positive attitude toward difficult or impossible odds" (page 24).

Personal Reflection and Recording

1. When did you first become aware of the Holy Spirit? What significance did this experience have upon you then?

2. What new understanding have you gained about the church, the Holy Spirit, and God's gifts?

3. What do you want to learn about the *charismata*?

4. Use a pencil or pen to draw your understanding of Christian ministry. Remember the empowering and creative power of God's Spirit!

These questions may be used for group reflection or conversation.

1. How does Paul define *charisma*? Try writing your answer in one sentence. How does this definition differ from contemporary understandings of *charisma*?

2. How do we acquire the gifts of the Spirit? What scripture passages support your answer? (See pages 18–19 in Bryant's book and 1 Cor. 12:6, 11, 28.)

3. How does Dr. Bryant understand the relationship between the effective use of the gifts and the growth and health of the church?

Practical Applications and Next Steps

Worship

During the next four services of worship, list the gifts being used and by whom. If those gifts are limited to the clergy or musicians, explore with the pastor what the church can do to involve more members in using their gifts in corporate worship. Explore with your pastor other ways to inform your church about the gifts of the Spirit and how these gifts can transform worship and bring renewal to the entire congregation and community.

The Bible

Start a new Bible study group or Sunday school class to study and learn about the gifts of the Spirit. Ask your pastor to teach a Bible study on the gifts before or during Pentecost.

Explore with the evangelism committee the possibility of offering a study of the gifts as a part of a new member training or orientation program. Perhaps this study of the gifts could be offered as a retreat for new church leadership. If this is not possible, in the next month share with at least two other persons what you have learned about the gifts.

Prayer

Let your observation of worship serve as a catalyst to begin a special prayer group to pray for your local church to become more open and accepting of the gifts of the Holy Spirit. Invite three other persons to join you in prayers for the church to discover or rediscover the gifts for growth and health. Agree on a specific length of time to pray for the church, such as seven to thirty days. Whenever possible, pray together as a group as well as individually.

Observe any changes of attitude, openness, renewed interest of the members of the congregation and pastoral staff. Share your observations with the members of the prayer group.

Witnessing

Name some of the responsibilities that we must consider as we use the gifts in Christ's name. What would diminish our witness for Christ?

Power

Talk with at least two members of your church about the power of God's gifts. You may wish to discuss these statements from Bryant's book:

1. "Each Christian has a personality or disposition colored by the specific gifts present and practiced. . . . Many Christians, if not most, practice their gifts without being consciously aware of them. Usually after two

years of growth, serious converts to Christ find a ministry consistent with their gifts—without knowing it. I have heard many persons tell how their work for Christ was joy-filled, but they didn't know why until they discovered that all along they were working out of their gifts" (pages 23–24).

2. ". . . God, not the individual or the community of Christians, chooses our gifts. . . . the biblical truth is that all Christians have spiritual gifts that carry extraordinary powers and responsibilities" (page 19).

Incomplete Data

List the information you need to grow and mature in your understanding of the gifts of the Holy Spirit. Tell a member of the group (as you feel comfortable) the steps that you are willing to take to achieve complete data concerning the gifts.

New Insight

List one new learning you have gained about the Holy Spirit that you feel is important and are willing to share with someone outside the study group.

Is It I, Lord?

1. In what new way or ways is God calling you to use your gifts, or *charismata*, in the ministry and mission of the church?

2. How is God calling you to help your congregation better understand and use the gifts of the Spirit?

Looking Ahead

In preparation for next time, think about members in the group you feel might be having difficulty in accepting the idea that they are gifted persons. Pray for them. Ask the Holy Spirit how you can be of help. Before reading chapter two, discover the topics that will be discussed as a quick way of seeing what the chapter is about.

Gifts of the Holy Spirit
A True / False Questionnaire

____ 1. Spiritual gifts are given only to the spiritually elite.

____ 2. The gifts of the Holy Spirit disappeared after the death of the last apostle.

____ 3. Gifts are given to every believer at his or her conversion.

____ 4. Speaking in tongues validates whether or not a person has been baptized in the Spirit.

____ 5. A person can possess all of the gifts.

____ 6. Gifts of the Spirit and the Fruit of the Spirit are one and the same.

____ 7. Gifts of the Spirit are given to empower believers to serve the church.

____ 8. Speaking in tongues is one of the spiritual gifts.

____ 9. A person can lose his or her gifts.

____10. Gifts may be thought of as the evangelistic tools of the church.

____11. All gifts of the Spirit have value and are necessary for the growth and health of the church.

____12. Gifts are given by God to accompany the new spiritual life of the believer.

____13. The apostle Paul listed all of the gifts of the Holy Spirit.

____14. When the gifts are either neglected or abused, the church becomes weak and ineffective.

____15. Now that the church has been established, the gifts are not relevant for today.

Answers

1. F; 2. F; 3. T; 4. T/F: For some, speaking in tongues may be the first sign of the presence of the Spirit, but this does not seem to be the norm today. 5. F; 6. F; 7. T; 8. T; 9.F; 10. T; 11. T; 12. T; 13. F; 14. T; 15. F.

SESSION TWO

The Source and Resources of Spiritual Gifts

Read aloud or have an individual read 1 Corinthians 12:4-6. Discuss the point that the gifts do not come from a human source, but from a spiritual source. Discuss what this means for the church today.

Ask the members to form small groups. Assign one of the five religious resources to each group for discussion. Have one person from each group report to the whole group (fifteen minutes).

Most gracious God, you are the source of all gifts. Your gifts often surprise us, but often we take your gifts for granted. Open us to sense your presence and your gifts. We thank you for gifts of the Spirit. We thank you for the gift of this time of study. We thank you for the resources of power you place before us. We thank you for persons who show us the way and who reveal your greater purposes for us and for the world. Gifts abound, O Lord. Awaken us to those gifts that reveal your love in Jesus Christ. Amen.

Charismata have a divine origin. Gifts endow believers with new abilities or powers to achieve effective service for the divine purpose. Gifts accompany the new spiritual life of the believer. They enable the Christian to share in the life, mission, and ministry of the resurrected Christ. Gifts are evangelistic resources to bring healing, wholeness, and salvation to a broken world.

Five Resources

Dr. Bryant lists five religious resources (available means) for spiritual gifts: worship, the Bible, prayer, witnessing, and power. What other resources for transformation in your community do you experience?

Worship

"The church at authentic worship requires the presence and operation of all the gifts, not just those operated by the minister and the musicians. When a church is so assembled, no force in the world can withstand its power for good (see Matt. 16:18). I submit that one way to restore to the church its effectiveness for peace and unity in the affairs of human beings is to discover and use the gifts. I contend further that one way to revitalize what, for many, has become dull and boring rituals of worship is to incorporate understanding, appreciation, and use of the gifts God has bestowed on us" (Bryant, page 28).

❧ When have you experienced relevant and exciting worship? How had you prepared for that worship?

The Bible

The Bible had little relevance before my conversion and subsequent baptism in the Holy Spirit. Yet, when I came alive in the Spirit, the Bible also came alive in a fresh new way. When we receive and use the gifts in accordance to their design and purposefulness, the Bible becomes a living study guide for holy and holistic living.

❦ When have you truly experienced the Bible as a living word rather than a collection of ancient texts?

Prayer

When a person is open to the gifts, that person will become aware of a new attraction to a deeper prayer life. Prayer takes on the character of a dialogue or communion with God. Prayers become more Christ-centered than self-centered. Prayer is a way of seeking to bring our wills into harmony with God's will.

Witnessing

In Acts 1:4-8, Jesus defined one role of the Holy Spirit as empowering believers to witness to his living presence in the world. Our gifts enable us to share in the mission and ministry of the risen Christ. Witnessing can take many forms, but the essence of authentic Christian witness is always motivated by love (agape). Deeds that produce health and wholeness in the body of Christ point to God.

Power

Jesus spoke of the Christian life as one of power in the Holy Spirit (John 14:12 and Acts 1:4-8). Jesus anticipated that the Holy Spirit would empower those who followed him to continue the public ministry of teaching, preaching, and healing. The power of the Holy Spirit would be manifested through the charismatic gifts for serving others in Christ's name (Rom. 12:1-8; 1 Cor. 12:1-31; Eph. 4:1-16; 1 Pet. 4:10-11; Heb. 2:4).

Our gifts unleash God's power for good in the world. The Spirit of God gives gifts to heal every kind of sickness and disease, as the shalom of God reaches all of humanity.

Invite persons to share with the group how their gifts have enhanced their prayer life. This is a good opportunity for you to share your experience of the importance of prayer (three to five minutes).

Ask persons to reflect on the five resources. Allow them to find a quiet place to do their reflection. Allow fifteen minutes. Then ask them to share their reflections in small groups of three or four and with the whole group.

Invite individuals to suggest other resources that are transformed through the presence and operation of the gifts.

List these on the chalkboard or newsprint to be used at a future time.

Stress that Jesus did not allow others to limit the gifts within him. We are to model our ministry after Jesus.

Personal Reflection and Recording

1. Think about your particular gifts in relation to your congregation or your family. What kinds of responses do people have toward your gifts? How do you feel about their responses?

2. As you reflect on the Gospels, how did people respond to Jesus' gifts? What Bible stories support your response?

3. How did Jesus respond to the rejections of others? What lessons should you learn from Jesus? What should the church learn from Jesus?

Help the group understand the necessity of dealing with prejudiced mindsets against persons who are different from themselves. Without openness to new experiences, we slow down the learning process of our own spiritual formation. Romans 12:1-2 reminds us of the importance of renewing our minds. This is to be a daily process of renewing our minds, if we are to discern God's will for our life each day and in each new situation.

Incomplete Data

What lesson does the parable of the good Samaritan teach you concerning the way you have in the past responded to the needs of persons different from yourself?

New Insight

Who do you identify with in the parable of the good Samaritan? Why?

Remind persons to do the reading before session three. Encourage them to note areas that they do not fully understand.

Looking Ahead

As you read the next chapter, seek God's power to witness lovingly to others about what you are learning.

Practical Applications and Next Steps

Jesus told the parable of the good Samaritan (Luke 10:25-37) to illustrate love in action toward others. According to Jesus, Christian love must be unselfish and unconditionally expressed to our neighbors near and far who are in need. Read this passage before you reflect on the following questions or suggestions.

Worship

Think about how your group might do a contemporary dramatization of Luke 10:25-37. What would be the setting of the episode? Who would be the contemporary victim of robbery? Who would be contemporary versions of the rabbi, the scribe, and the Samaritan? How could such a dramatization during worship challenge you and your congregation to become more responsive to other people, particularly persons not in your congregation?

The Bible

How does this parable help you understand that all people are your neighbors? List one or two ministries of your congregation that meet specific needs of persons in your community. What new ways of ministry do you envision for your church?

Prayer

How does the parable of the good Samaritan change your prayer life? Write a prayer in this workbook based on the parable. Write a prayer that asks for God's help to meet a special need in your community. Ask God to reveal the gifts within you that can bring God's love to this situation.

Witnessing

Recall a situation or event when you reached out to help someone in need when others had failed to help. How did the other person feel? How did you feel?

Ask the group to read Luke 10:25-37, the parable of the good Samaritan, and to apply this story to the five resources: Worship, the Bible, Prayer, Witnessing, and Power.

As persons discuss the dramatization of the verses in Luke 10, relax them by interjecting humor or playfulness. One of the unique characteristics of the Christian life is joy.

Close the session by reading together the prayer on page 20. Determine whether individuals would like to compose a prayer for use during worship. Offer the prayer as a gift from the study group to the congregation.

Power

What gifts did the good Samaritan discover within himself? How are these gifts needed in the contemporary church? How do those gifts manifest God's power in the world?

Is It I, Lord?

What area in your life needs anointing and binding from a good Samaritan? What would strengthen you so that you can reach out to meet the needs of hurting persons in your congregation, community, or family?

SESSION THREE

What the Spiritual Gifts Are Not

Gracious God, we give you thanks and praise for your many gifts. These gifts make visible your love, presence, grace, and power. Help us to accept all the gifts and graces that you lavish upon us. We celebrate their rich diversity. We thank you for sending your son Jesus Christ, who is the ultimate gift of salvation. Bless this session and our time together. In the name of Jesus Christ and through the presence and power of Your Holy Spirit we pray. Amen.

> *Now concerning spiritual gifts, brothers and sisters, I do not want you to be uninformed (1 Corinthians 12:1, NRSV).*

Charles Bryant and I hope in our workshops and in these books to clarify the confusion that exists about spiritual gifts. We both experience the difficulty of having first to define the gifts in the negative way in order to explain what the *charismata* are not!

Spiritual Gifts Are Not Skills or Natural Talents

How do you distinguish between your natural abilities or talents and your spiritual gifts? How do your spiritual gifts empower your ministry? How does your church call on you to use your spiritual gifts as well as your natural talents?

Some people confuse grace-gifts with natural talents or abilities. Acknowledging our talents is one of the ways God is saying that gifts are present within us. The Holy Spirit passes on the charismata through our conversion or new spiritual birth. James reminds us that all gifts, both natural (ordinary) and supernatural (extraordinary) come from God (James 1:17). We are to thank God for them and to celebrate their purposefulness.

Christians do not have an unfair advantage over non-Christians when it comes to their physical, mental, academic, and social skills. God gives talents to accompany the human life. They enhance the human quality of life in the physical world.

Begin by praying this prayer together.

Provide time before the session begins for persons to share new learnings, concerns, and testimonies.

Use a small piece of hose and a two-feet piece of string to illustrate how our natural talents are conduits for our grace-gifts. The hose represents our talent or ordinary gifts. The string (or water) passing through the hose represents the gift.

It may help to think of human talents as ordinary gifts and grace-gifts as extraordinary gifts.

Charismata are more than our natural talents. The Bible states that *charismata* add a new dimension unique to the spiritual life of the believer. Grace-gifts or *charismata* are not limited to, or governed by, the physical or material world as are natural talents. *Charismata* point us to our spiritual origin.

Dr. Bryant presents a practical way of understanding the relationship between natural abilities and *charismata*. He believes that one's natural talent or skill is a means for the operation of *charisma* (grace-gift). Bryant rightly gives a special place and value to both our natural talents and our grace-gifts. God uses our natural talents and abilities to transport *charismata*. They are intimately and interdependently connected, but are uniquely different (see page 35).

We can use both our natural gifts and grace-gifts to serve others in Christ's name. God calls us to dedicate all that we have and all that we are in God's service.

Spiritual Gifts Are Not Roles

The old model for the church assigned ministry to professionals. Exploring the spiritual gifts clarifies the reality that all the people of God are gifted for ministry.

We must change our attitude in the way we define ministry and how we relate to people in ministry. Jesus said that the coming of the Holy Spirit would empower all God's people to witness to his presence in the world after his resurrection. Each person's gifts are different and have different functions in the body of Christ, to manifest the kingdom of God and to uniquely bring God's kingdom into daily life. I strongly believe that our gifts are of no real value if they do not enable all believers to make real the kingdom of God, in everyday life, for all people.

Spiritual Gifts Are Not Offices

Dr. Bryant makes the following statement: "The office does not automatically guarantee the extraordinary power of the Spirit that energizes the gift. In the earliest Christian communities there is evidence that without rank and status, even education (see Acts 4:13), certain persons surfaced with extraordinary abilities and insight for the church's development. Paul described this phenomenon as grace for edifying and building up the fellowship. The persons had no titles, since organization was not the purpose of their work" (pages 37–38).

❧ Use one word to describe how you respond to Bryant's belief that "it is imperative for us [the body of Christ] to reintroduce the ministries after the example of our Lord, [which are] to be lived out in unselfish dedication, compassion, and spiritually directed service" (page 39).

❧ Now draw a picture of what Bryant's statement means for your congregation.

Spiritual Gifts Are Not the Fruit of the Spirit.

People often confuse the fruit and the gifts of the Spirit, but they are not the same. Galatians 5:22 describes the fruit of the Spirit as love, joy, peace, patience, kindness, goodness, faithfulness, gentleness, and self-control. These fruits define the Christlike character of the Christian. As a follower of Jesus grows in grace, these virtues are the products of a Christ-filled, Christ-empowered life.

C. Peter Wagner distinguishes between gifts as task-oriented and fruit as God-oriented in his book *Your Spiritual Gifts Can Help Your Church Grow*. Wagner also points out that gifts are temporal while fruit, growing out of agape, has an eternal quality. Love demands that Christians seek the gifts for ministry for the good of and on behalf of others. Our gifts express agape love.

❧ Draw or write your response to the following statement: Love is a prerequisite to the proper and effective operation of the gifts of the Spirit.

Spiritual Gifts Are Not for Self-Gain

If possible, read Romans 12:3 in different versions.

> . . . *Do not think of yourself more highly than you ought, but rather think of yourself with sober judgment, in accordance with the measure of faith God has given you (Romans 12:3).*

Spiritual pride, misuse, selfish gain, and neglect of the gifts can destroy the body of Christ. When we mutually use the gifts for the common good of all, the church grows and matures as God intends. The New Testament asserts that Christians are stewards of their grace-gifts (1 Pet. 4:10).

Remember that the fruit of the Spirit is the normal, expected end of Christian growth. This Christlike character develops within the Christian as he or she abides in Christ (John 15).

No single gift defines a Christian's life or life in the Spirit; it is defined by a "love-empowered" life serving others.

Help the group to understand that the gifts can function without the fruit, but the gifts will not produce the intended result of helping the church to grow and mature as God intends.

Form small groups and ask several persons to read aloud Matthew 25:14-30. Ask them to discuss the three questions in the text (ten minutes).

Encourage the group to share as much as they are comfortable with another person.

❧ What does it mean to be a steward of God's gifts?

❧ How is your faithfulness in using your gifts related to success?

❧ How would you respond if God asked you, "What did you do with the *charismata* I gave you?"

Ask the group what the church would look like if everyone had the same gifts.

Conclude this section by reading aloud page 42, Bryant. Ask the group to respond to the question in the main text.

Spiritual Gifts Are Not the Same for Everyone

No biblical evidence suggests that one person possesses all the gifts, but biblical evidence supports the idea that gifts are unique to each person. The gifts are different for each person. Each believer has been given a specific ministry-gift or ministry-task in the body of Christ. Paul wrote the Corinthians that the whole body should not be like a single part (1 Cor. 12) because the body would cease to function as God intended. The gifts are different for each individual, and the gifts complement one another.

❧ If the Bible offers no hint of biblical proof that a person can possess all the available gifts, or that any of the gifts is for every person, how can we answer the person who says that all of the gifts are within every Christian?

Remind participants that we must discover, develop, and learn how to use the gifts. This process is necessary to use our gifts effectively.

Gifts Are Not Given Fully Developed

Our gifts and spiritual abilities are not given to us fully developed. We must grow into our gifts. When we receive the gifts, however, they already have all the power or energy to fulfill God's purposes. Yet, we must discover the nature and scope of our gifts. We must grow into our gifts and allow them to fully develop in us through faithful use. The more we use our gifts, study them, talk about them, and even experiment with them, the more confidence we will gain in using them.

Personal Reflection and Recording

1. How is the Holy Spirit helping you to get more in touch with your grace-gifts?
2. How do you feel about the fact that God has assigned certain gifts to you for the health and growth of the body of Christ?

Practical Applications and Next Steps

Worship

Make a special effort during the next Sunday worship service to thank God for giving gifts to the church as a means of guaranteeing its well being.

The Bible

Read Ephesians 4:1-14. Note anything that strikes you as important and needed today concerning the unity of the body.

Prayer

Pray for your pastor to discover the *charismata* to help the church to grow.

Witnessing

How does accepting your responsibility to help each member of the body of Christ to grow in faith witness to the Lordship of Christ in your Christian walk?

Power

How do you understand God's power at work in the health and growth of your congregation? of your denomination? of the church around the world?

Incomplete Data

What new insight about the *charismata* did your receive?

New Insight

What talent, skill, or ability has the Holy Spirit revealed to you that you need to use to allow certain gifts to flow through you? How will this change or empower you to serve others better?

Is It I, Lord?

What gift or gifts is God confirming within you to help the church grow? What gift or gifts is God calling you to lay down for your growth?

How is your church calling you to use your new gifts?

Looking Ahead

Study chapter four in Bryant's book before the next gathering. How do you define the gifts of the Holy Spirit?

Close this session with the Lord's Prayer.

SESSION FOUR

What the Spiritual Gifts Are

Open with this prayer or pray in your own words.

Begin this session by reading aloud 1 Corinthians 2:9-10.

Let the group respond to the following statement:
Each gift has a unique function and a specific purpose.

Gracious God, we thank and praise you for your presence among us. We celebrate your presence. We thank you for Jesus Christ. We celebrate our oneness in Jesus Christ and the unity that the Holy Spirit brings in our midst. Help us to reach out to one another with the love, compassion, and power that Christ gives. Open us to discover our gifts to bring your healing grace to others. Empower us to see with clear vision and to discover new ways to minister in Christ's name. Amen.

> *No eye has seen, no ear has heard, no mind has conceived what God has prepared for those who love him but God has revealed it to us by his Spirit (1 Corinthians 2:9-10).*

Spiritual Gifts Are Unmerited Blessings from God

If we were to list all the gifts or blessings we receive from God, the list would have no end. The Bible tells us that God finds great joy and keen pleasure in bestowing divine blessings upon us. We can see this in God's blessing of Abraham and Sarah and those who followed in the biblical history. God's blessings pass down to those who enter into covenant with God. God's nature is to bless us. God's love and grace are free, and know no bounds. Grace is God's redemptive love in action, the unmerited favor, which God extends to all people.

Dr. Bryant states that unmerited grace does not mean unneeded grace. Everyone needs God's love and grace. Both are essential for our salvation. Both are necessary to experience the abundant life, which Jesus Christ makes possible (John 10:10). Saving grace is the same for each person, but serving grace is different from one person to another.

Charismata empower believers to share in the life, mission, and ministry of the risen Christ. Bryant offers keen insight into the psychological and social blessings that accompany God's assignment of a gift. He points out the following:

1. The recipients become motivated to do everything possible with their gifts as an expression of gratitude in faithful service to God.

2. Recipients never consider themselves in competition with others in the body of Christ (1 Cor. 13:4-5).
3. Faithful handling of the gifts brings such joy and power that the recipients never experience burnout.

Spiritual Gifts Are Job Descriptions for Ministry

God did not save us just for heaven. God's salvation is an expression of divine love, grace, and mercy. God's saving grace is something we can experience daily as we walk with Christ and abide in his love.

C. Peter Wagner has written extensively about the spiritual dynamics of the gifts and relates them to church growth. He has written about the dynamic movement of the Holy Spirit among people in third-world countries. He attributes the powerful way God draws people into the Kingdom by the authoritative manifestation of gifts of the Spirit in these nations. Dr. Bryant reminds us that God is bringing about wholeness, righteousness, and justice in the world through the presence and employment of gifts.

Invite individuals to share some of their experiences in using the gifts.

Find out if any of their experiences confirm the three blessings suggested by Bryant.

What else have group participants experienced?

❧ How do the gifts help the church witness to Christ's continuous presence in the world?

❧ What would be different if the gifts were absent?

Spiritual Gifts Are a Means for Discovering God's Will

Stumbling through life without direction, purpose, or meaning can rob a person of living a satisfying and productive Christian life. The apostle Paul reminds us that our gifts "prove what is the will of God, what is good and acceptable and perfect" (Rom. 12:2, RSV). What could be more meaningful and satisfying than to discover your gifts and calling in life. We know from experience that few activities can be more confusing and disheartening than working or serving in the church without knowing God's will.

◊ When have you experienced this confusing clash? Did you experience it as a test of faith or as a reason to ask deeper questions of your faith life?

◊ How did you grow in your awareness of your spiritual gifts?

Spiritual Gifts Are Guarantees of Effective Service

The gifts are guarantees of effective and efficient services to the church and through the church to the world. The essence of the *charismata* is God's gift of God's self-revealing presence to bring health and salvation to a sinful and broken world.

One of the ways to assure effective service in the body of Christ comes from all gifts working together for the health and vitality of the church. Each person must see his or her gift working interdependently with all of the other gifts for the good of the entire body.

Dr. Bryant writes that we must find the proper place to do God's will: "We need to recognize other members' place and the value of their gifts. Effectiveness in sustaining fellowship and outreach ministries comes from all gifts working together in mutual interdependence" (page 47).

The church must find meaningful and creative ways to match the gifts of persons with the time they can give to ministry. The church must provide settings in which members of the congregation can share with one another the unique aspects of their spiritual journey.

Gifts work best within the mission and ministry of the local church. The Bible warns against persons not regularly assembling together as the church, the body of Christ. Bryant writes:

"They [church members who stay away from worship] deny an integral aspect of the divine nature of the church, which is *koinonia* (fellowship). . . . This type of fellowship makes the church different from any other human effort" (page 48).

When you discover your gifts, you will never be the same. You will come alive in a new way. I experienced great joy when I discovered my grace-gifts. The church too has come alive through my gifts.

Personal Reflection and Recording

If you did not have grace-gifts, what difference would it make? Would it change your life? How would it affect the church?

Read aloud this quotation from page 47, and allow time for the group to discuss their feelings about this statement. How much of the effectiveness of the gifts depends on us? the Lord?

Practical Applications and Next Steps

Worship

What gifts or talents do you offer as an act of worship to God?

The Bible

Read 1 Peter 4:10-11. How does the letter writer understand the responsibility of the Christian as stewards of the gifts? the efficient service of the gifts?

Prayer

Some theologians see a close relationship between prayer and ministry and burnout. Without prayer, the acts of ministry cause spiritual and psychological burnout. What do you think and feel about this statement?

How will you help those around you maintain a life of prayer?

Witnessing

Read Matthew 25:14-30. Draw stick figures to illustrate this parable and your response to it.

As you recall the parable of the talents (Matt. 25:14-30), which character represents the majority of your congregation? Why?

Power

1. Do you feel empowered by God for ministry after worship? after private prayer? What would help you feel God's power for ministry?

2. If you work with people, do you feel God's power for witness when you are with them? Do you feel confident to talk about matters that are of ultimate importance?

3. What has God given to Christians that has the potential of releasing that power for good?

Incomplete Data

What idea, concept, belief, behavior, or attitude have you changed since beginning this session? Why?

New Insight

In what way do you consider the following statement helpful in understanding the nature and scope of the gifts? The local church that discovers its gifts will also find that its health and growth depends on all gifts. How do you see God using your gifts to achieve this end?

Is It I, Lord?

What new awareness have you gained about the relationship between prayer and ministry? How will you use it?

Looking Ahead

Read chapter five in Bryant's book. Jot down any questions raised by the material that require further explanation. Bring the questions before the group for discussion.

SESSION FIVE

Varieties of Gifts, Services, and Results

O God, breathe on us with the breath of abundant life. Breathe on us that we may experience your Spirit new, fresh, wondrous. Empower us to inhale the life-giving sustenance. Empower us to exhale all that feels stale and worn. Refresh us with your Spirit that we may commit ourselves anew to Jesus Christ and that we may sense our commission to go forth to all the world for Jesus' sake. Amen.

Pray this prayer together.

Give special time for those persons who might have questions from the reading in chapter 5.

> *Now there are varieties of gifts, but the same Spirit; and there are varieties of services, but the same Lord; and there are varieties of activities, but it is the same God who activates all of them in everyone (1 Cor. 12:4-6, NRSV).*

Paul's teachings were not intended to introduce a comprehensive list of the gifts. His teachings were in response to particular and unique historical situations. He intended to correct a divisive notion that only some Christians were gifted with spiritual gifts. Paul argued that no gifts were dispensable and that all believers were both spiritual and gifted.

Dr. Bryant notes twenty-one gifts identified in the early church (page 51), but he reminds us that the list of gifts is as limitless as God's love. We cannot try to enclose God's creativity with our limited understanding.

Five Schools of Thought

Scholars identify other New Testament ministries that they believe constitute *charismata* not named by Paul. Dr. Bryant identifies five schools of thought that attempt to understand, number, and identify the gifts:

1. The gifts no longer exist today and all the *charismata* ceased with the death of the apostles. Try to name a person or a group who you know that fits in this category.
2. Some gifts remain today, but other gifts such as miracles and healing ended immediately after the birth of the church. How do you respond to this thought?
3. Only some persons possess and use the *charismata*. How do you respond to this claim?
4. All Christian believers receive all of the gifts, and the circumstances of the believer determines which gifts to use. How do you respond to this idea?

5. All gifts are necessary and are as valid today as they were in the early church.

Dr. Bryant writes: "I refuse to believe we know all there is to know about God and the gifts of the Spirit (see 1 Cor. 2:10). I do not believe the Bible contains all God has to reveal. I believe God is so limitless and all-loving that the abundant life Jesus offers in John 10:10 is far more than we could ever imagine" (page 52).

Thus the gifts are as relevant today as they were in the early church. They communicate Christ's presence in the church today.

Read aloud Bryant's statement and continue on to page 53. Invite the participants to discuss what they feel Bryant means about the sacramental nature of the gifts.

Classification of Gifts

Some people classify gifts as speaking gifts, serving gifts, sign gifts. In *The Gifts of the Spirit* Harold Horton suggests that the gifts fit naturally into three groups: (1) gifts of revelation, (2) gifts of power, and (3) gifts of inspiration. How have you tried to classify God's gifts?

Application

The gifts are given by God to carry out God's divine purposes for creation and salvation. There is no limit to the numerous ways that gifts may be employed in serving the church for growth, health, and maturity. The essential purpose of the gifts is to bring justice, health, wholeness, and righteousness to all the world.

Read aloud the statement from Bryant's book, page 55, about the purpose of the gifts. Ask the group to respond to the statement. What does this statement mean for the church today?

Think of a creative ministry in your community. What gifts for justice, wholeness, and righteousness do you witness in that ministry?

Expectations

Most of us can take comfort in knowing that our gifts do not entirely depend on us. The Holy Spirit enables us to do more than we can do and to be more than we are. Jesus says this best in John 15:5b: ". . . apart from me you can do nothing" (NRSV). The Spirit bestows gifts upon us and also operates these gifts in and through us as we seek to fulfill God's call to ministry. Knowing this should encourage us to let our expectations soar to new heights and wonders.

Close this section by reading Bryant's thoughtful perspective about the expectation of the gifts on pages 55–57.

Personal Reflection and Recording

Read the four main passages dealing with the gifts: Romans 12:6-8, 27-30; 1 Corinthians 12:8-11; Ephesians 4:6-8; 1 Peter 4:10-11. Note carefully all of the gifts. Make a list of the gifts you have used at one time or another. In using those gifts, which of them gives the greatest satisfaction or makes you feel good in serving others?

Practical Applications and Next Steps

Worship

Adopt an Old Testament ritual: Build a simple altar to God and recognize the gifts you have received from God for ministry. The ritual may be as simple as lighting a candle during your devotional time and giving thanks to God marking this special event. You may wish to speak during public worship and offer the testimony to acknowledge your gifts and dedicate them for the good of the church and to the glory of God.

The Bible

Read 1 Corinthians 12:4-31. What does it mean to be the body of Christ today?

Draw a picture of the body of Christ as you experience it. (Or if you wish, write a song or poem about the body of Christ.)

Prayer

Offer prayers for the leaders of the church of Jesus Christ. Remember bishops, national church staff, district superintendents or associate ministers, pastors, and other leaders. Pray that God will open their hearts to the work and ministries of the Holy Spirit. Pray that they will value the *charismata* as a means to bring lasting growth and health to the body of Christ. Encourage those in your church who have this concern to pray this prayer throughout the next year.

Witnessing

What *charismata* can you begin to see in yourself in response to the needs of others? How are you witnessing to the God's grace working in you?

Power

How might you use your gifts to bring God's healing and wholeness to your church community?

Spend time in small groups sharing your responses to questions in "Pratical Applications and Next Steps."

See Genesis 28:18-22 as an example of making a simple altar to God. This act of worship is to give thanks to the graciousness of God for your grace-gifts. This will serve as a landmark in your life and ministry in the service of God.

Incomplete Data

With which school of thought on the *charismata* do you feel most comfortable? What changes have you made concerning your understanding of the gifts? Name attitudes or concerns that block you from using your gifts.

New Insight

1. List two things you have learned about the gifts that will help you use your gifts more effectively in serving the church and the world.

2. Reread Romans 12:2. How do you understand the relationship between living a transformed life and the need for cultivating a renewed mind?

Is It I, Lord?

What vision is developing within you that gives you hope for a relevant and healthy future church? How is God calling you to work or to pray for the reality of this church?

Looking Ahead

Close the session by singing one of the songs of praise in your congregation's hymnal.

Session Six is a very long session with a wealth of material. You need a plan. Consider the suggestions stated in the section "Leaders" (pages 8–9) or the following. First study those gifts you think you have received. Next, study those gifts that interest you the most. Then study those gifts that you want to learn more about, or those that you discover when you complete the Twelve-Step Self-Evaluation to Discover Your Gifts (Appendix).

SESSION SIX

A Gift Is a Gift Is a Gift Is a Gift

Eternal God, your love prods and pushes us, lighting fires deep within us, ordering our lives within the mission of Jesus Christ. Eternal God, your loving example inspires us. We witness your mighty acts of giving throughout history, and we witness your gifts in those who have gone before us. Now enable us to know and understand your gifts, and knowing these gifts, help us to identify and develop those gifts so that our gifts may bless others and proclaim your love to a world in need. In Jesus' name we pray. Amen.

But to all who received him, who believed in his name, he gave power to become children of God, who were born, not of blood or of the will of the flesh or of the will of man, but of God. And the Word became flesh and lived among us, and we have seen his glory (John 1:12-14, NRSV).

Remember that a person's gift is not a sign of their spirituality. Please feel free to study more about those gifts that interest you. The gifts are listed alphabetically.

Introduction

If the gifts promote growth, health, and unity in the body of Christ, they are authentic. If growth, health, and unity are not apparent in the church, test the Spirit to learn what is being said to the church. Spiritual gifts do not bring disunity within the body of Christ; *charismata* are given to build up the church. Gifts do not make anyone a super Christian, but gifts make us better than we would be without them.

Jesus chose twelve very ordinary persons: uneducated, poor, fishermen, tax collectors, probably farmers, and an activist. Jesus still chooses very ordinary people like you and me to receive gifts to proclaim God's love. Like the first disciples, we probably find it difficult to believe that we have gifts to heal and reveal the presence of God's kingdom.

In your congregation you will discover gifted individuals. Some have gifts for teaching, healing, encouraging, leading, showing compassion, and giving. Others are given gifts for singing, praying, exhorting, inspiring, visioning, showing mercy, speaking in tongues, and prophesying. Still others have

Pray together and then sing or read a hymn such as "Of All the Spirit's Gifts to Me" or "Breathe on Me, Breath of God."

Note that the acceptance and faithful use of the gifts distinguish between church membership and authentic discipleship.

Remember that the gifts accompany the new spiritual life of the believer.

gifts for believing, empowering, giving words of wisdom, evangelizing, or doing many other useful ministries that God envisions as needs to bring wholeness and salvation to people.

We receive our spiritual gifts when we experience the spiritual new birth. God alone assigns the gifts to us, and places us in the context of life where we can best discover our gifts, use them, and develop them for the needs of others. I am thankful that God has the responsibility for working out all of the details. Not only does God know me better than I know myself, God knows what gifts best fit me psychologically, emotionally, and spiritually. And God understands you in the same ways.

Keep in mind that the definitions do not include how a particular gift might influence other gifts. Each gift is unique; however, a companion gift may uniquely alter it. Be aware that no two gifts conflict; but always complement each other. Gifts are like individual pieces of a puzzle. Each gift has a unique place in the body of Christ, and each makes up the whole of the body.

Administration

. . . those with gifts of administration . . . (1 Corinthians 12:28).

Administration comes from the Greek word *kubernesis* and describes the position and responsibility of a pilot or helmsman of a ship. A helmsman is one who determines the direction of the whole vessel. It is a directional and managerial ministry. The administrator can often see the complete picture of where the church has been, where it is, and the direction it must engage in to have a vital and effective ministry.

❧ How does the image of a pilot describe one you know as an administrator?

❧ How do you consider the gift of administration among your own gifts?

Pay special attention to administration and to the particular gifts of those in this study. Challenge the group to learn all they can about these gifts.

Challenge persons on nominating committees to seek persons with the gifts suited for appropriate ministries. Explore what the church might look like today if we would match the gifted person to the needs of the church.

Apostle

"It was he who gave some to be apostles . . . (Ephesians 4:11).

Some people would say that the gift of apostleship is long past. I do not believe that this is true and agree with Dr. Bryant on this point. I met an anointed and gifted brother in the Lord from Harare, Zimbabwe, whom I consider to be a modern day apostle. His name is Ezekiel Guti. Guti takes the message of the gospel to people who have not heard it and has established a vast ministry in Zimbabwe and beyond. His ministry has at least a million members. He continues to establish new churches. He has the oversight for a thousand or more pastors. Guti trains and appoints pastors to serve the churches he establishes. He has also established Bible schools to train pastors. These facets of Guti's ministry help me think of him as a contemporary apostle.

❡ How do you respond to apostleship as a gift of the Spirit? Can you identify a contemporary apostle?

Battle

For our struggle is not against flesh and blood, but. . . . against the powers of this dark world and against the spiritual forces of evil in the heavenly realms (Ephesians 6:12).

The Bible comprises many narratives of Spirit-empowered persons gifted to engage in battle against evil forces and against persons who embody evil. The apostle Paul strongly believed that God empowers persons in the church to expose and to destroy the works of evil that seek to hinder or frustrate God's people from carrying out the purposes of God.

Evil forces are running rampant in the world and are not excluded from the church. The church remains in a constant battle against evil both inside and outside. God makes available all of the power and spiritual resources necessary to confront and defeat the forces and forms of evil as often as we face them.

❡ Jesus understood that part of his mission was to destroy the powers of evil. He fully anticipated that his followers would continue his mission of combating the evil forces of Satan. When have you battled forces of evil?

Remind the group that the Bible does not support the notion that any of the gifts have passed away, but that new gifts are added. Help individuals to work through their feelings concerning contemporary apostles.

Remind the participants that the Bible contains many accounts of Spirit-empowered individuals who do battle against evil and persons who embody evil.

Ask the group to discuss the responsibility of each Christian to win and never lose in a confrontation with evil.

Craftsmanship

Read the passage in Exodus and the statement from the main text (page 67).

Read Exodus 35:25, 30-33 for a biblical account of craftsmaking.

Our gifts in God's hands becomes unlimited creative resources. Dr. Bryant defines craftsmanship as "the extraordinary ability to use physical materials and artistic skills to create, mold, carve, sculpt, draw, design, paint, repair, or photograph items necessary for spiritual nurture, faith development, and caring ministries" (page 67). This spiritual gift can communicate the Gospel to those who learn nonverbally. The challenge for the church is to encourage those with the gift of crafts to discover how their gifts serve God. Consider what a person with the gift of crafts might do in teaching about the love of God while teaching a skill to a group of adults or a group of children. At the heart of such activity is caring and spiritual nurture.

Think about how your church's ministry may grow through the gift of crafts.

Discerning of the Spirits

. . . to another the ability distinguishing between spirits . . . (1 Corinthians. 12:10).

The gift of discernment (Greek, *diakrisis*) is the ability to distinguish between spirits to determine whether they originate from the divine, human, or demonic. The aim is always to protect the integrity of the church and to keep the church from moving out of God's plan and will. This gift helps the church sift through confusing doctrines, teachings, theologies, philosophies, and grandiose schemes.

Discernment can work on various levels. Discernment is maintaining a balanced perspective from God's viewpoint. A second level of discernment is the ability to know whether a thing done by a person comes from a godly motive or a carnal motive. A third level of discernment is the ability to determine truth from error, even though the motives may be proper.

Remember the following characteristics of authentic discerners:

1. Authentic discerners are not quick to judge behavior or programs that claim to be God's will and tend to be very sensitive to spiritual matters.
2. People often misunderstand discerners because they think all discerners are introverts. Discerners, however, include all personality types. Discerners judge issues with their hearts rather than their heads. If you want to know how to settle a deeply divided group, test the feelings of persons with the gift of discernment.

My friend Danny Morris believes that the church must become a discerning body. Decisions affecting church life and policy must be done by a discernment process rather than a process based on parliamentary procedure. The church is a theocracy, not a democracy, and must adopt a system of decision making that produces community, harmony, and the shalom of God.

❦ How have you tried to discern God's will for your congregation?

Stress that the gift of discernment is given to protect the integrity of the church as it seeks to judge and to fulfill the will of God.

How do group members try to discern the will of God? How does your church try to discern the will of God?

Evangelism

. . . some to be evangelists . . . (Ephesians 4:11).

The gift of evangelism offers visible results now and in the future. Ask participants what they consider to be the problem with evangelism.

Evangelism stems from the Greek root *euangelizamai,* meaning "to declare," "to announce," "to proclaim," or "to present good news to win persons to Christ."

The New Testament evangelist is not the caricature that contemporary society portrays. An authentic evangelist proclaims a message of God's love, grace, and mercy to people in need of redemption.

The call to evangelism is not the exclusive work of the evangelists. Every believer in the body of Christ has a "common anointing" to tell others the good news of Jesus Christ. We serve a God who loves and seeks the lost, an evangelistic God. Love compels us to share our faith, to tell others what God has done. These actions fulfill the great commission.

Most people deny that they have the gift of evangelism. Many lay persons probably deny this calling because they believe that evangelism is a ministry for the ordained ministers only. Remember that all renewal movements are led by the people of the church. The challenge for the church today is to rediscover the ministry of evangelism and to provide every opportunity for those who have this gift to use it for the glory of God. Evangelism is the mission of the whole church (Acts 1:8).

Personal Reflection and Recording

In the space below, reflect on your understanding of the grace-gifts just discussed—administration, apostle, battle, craftmanship, discernment, and evangelism. Pay special attention to those gifts that interest you. Keep a list of these gifts that interest you or give you a feeling of joy.

Ask persons to reflect individually on the four questions in the main text. Then ask them to share their reflections in their small group and / or whole group.

1. What surprises did you experience doing this portion of the study?

2. Which of your gifts have received affirmation from others? Are you discovering your grace-gifts? What is your next step?

3. How is Jesus calling you to use your gifts for ministry today?

4. What reservations do you have?

Remind the group that they should approach this section with enthusiasm and joy.

Personal Applications and Next Steps

Worship

What work of grace in your life and ministry can you celebrate and give thanks to God? Share this with your prayer partner. Take this opportunity to dedicate your gifts for the service of Christ.

The Bible

Read 1 Corinthians 13 several times, preferably in a translation that is not familiar to you. Explore Paul's theological understanding of the importance of love in using the *charismata*.

1. What is Paul saying to the Christians in Corinth? to the church today?

2. Why is love at the center of the gospel? Why should love be at the center of everything Christians do in word or deed?

3. How has the Holy Spirit empowered you to serve others?

Prayer

How are you allowing the discipline of prayer to deepen your relationship with the Holy Spirit?

Witnessing

What does it mean to be a gifted Christian in the world today? How do gifts empower Christians to witness to Christ's compassion and love?

Power

John Wesley understood each Christian to be a gifted minister—responsible for seeing the gospel proclaimed in word and deed. How is God empowering the church to do battle against evil and win with good?

Incomplete Data

Have you discovered any of the following gifts in your everyday life?
1. Apostle

2. Battle

3. Craftsmanship

4. Discernment

5. Evangelism

6. Administration

New Insight

How would you describe the work of the Holy Spirit in your life today as related to the *charismata*?

Draw a picture of the faith community in ministry. You may cut pictures from magazines to make a montage to depict the community in ministry. Display the montage for others in the congregation to see.

Enjoy this important activity.

Is It I, Lord?

What new direction is God calling the church toward today? What is your Christian response to the needs you see in the world? How has God gifted you to minister to some of these needs?

Ask if anyone would like to offer a testimony or ask a question about the gifts.

Exhortation

. . . the exhorter, in exhortation . . . (Romans 12:8 NRSV).

Have you met persons who are always pleasant and speak encouraging words? Does your spirit feel uplifted in their presence? Those gifted persons fit the description of persons with the gift of exhortation. Exhortation consists of two parts: call and companionship. These persons are called to help persons develop positive attitudes and feelings about themselves and their relationship with God.

The task of the exhorter is to bring encouragement and comfort to others. Dr. Bryant reminds us that the church needs to discover persons like Barnabas, who encouraged others. He inspired others to take seriously their discipleship and to work hard in the ministry of the church.

Ask the group to write in the margin of their workbook the names of persons they know who have the gift of exhortation.

❧ What would you do with this gift if it were yours?

Ask individuals what they feel and think should be the role of the church in addressing exorcism?

Ask individuals to share their reponses to this question: How is Christ calling the church to confront the evil that is trying to destroy the world?

Stress again that the ultimate purpose of the gifts is to bring growth and health to the body of Christ.

Read aloud the statement from Bryant's book, page 80.

Exorcism

When Jesus had called the Twelve together, he gave them power and authority to drive out all demons and to cure diseases . . . (Luke 9:1).

One of the most misunderstood of all the gifts among Protestant Christians is exorcism. Many people are still greatly influenced by the worldview of Aristotle which strongly rejects anything that has to do with the spiritual realm. Or they are influenced by the motion picture industry.

Exorcism landed Paul and Silas in jail, but Paul does not list it as a *charisma*. The word *exorcism* is not specifically found in the Bible. Yet, Christians should not be surprised that God equips and empowers the body of Christ with the gift of exorcism. Jesus and his followers brought healing and wholeness to persons possessed by demons or evil spirits.

Exorcism comes from the Greek word *exorkistes*. It means "to drive out," "to expel," "to release," "to call forth," or "to free." Bryant defines exorcism as "the ability to use various means of faith, prayers, spirit-music, and other gifts to liberate persons from evil-centered hindering forces so that they may be in effective ministry to and for the body of Christ" (page 81). The person with this gift does not necessarily possess all these gifts but is able to use these gifts for the exorcising operation. The gift of discernment usually accompanies the gift of exorcism. When healing comes through exorcism, many of the other gifts are part of this healing process.

Many psychiatrists and psychologists are challenging the body of Christ not to overlook the potential good offered through exorcism. Psychiatrists and psychologists "have discovered illnesses of mind and powers that cripple and destroy for which there is no physical explanation or cure apart from spiritual realities. The New Testament contains many illustrations and descriptions of exorcism. Yet, a large segment of Christianity remains silent and indifferent toward this subject" (Bryant, page 80).

❧ How can the church take seriously the power God has given to defeat the evil forces which seek to destroy or distort God's good creation?

Tell the group that with the restoration of this gift, more people will be set free from the enslavement of demonic influence and activity.

Persons with the gift of exorcism have no delusion that their human power equals the power of evil. They do not attempt to minister alone. The Gospels point out that even Jesus sent his disciples out two by two to heal the sick and to cast out demons.

Once I was part of a group praying for a woman with a demonic possession. The demon spoke to us with a man's voice through this person and said to me, "I know who you are. You have no power over us." This puzzled us because this experience was new. After praying for divine guidance, I blurted out, "I know that we do not have power over you, in and of ourselves, but in the name of Jesus, I bind your power over this person. I command you to loose your hold over her and set her free. Come out of her now in the name of Jesus." As we watched the woman's face, her countenance began to change. We knew that God had given us the victory. We prayed for three hours for this person's complete deliverance. The woman was gloriously set free from demon influence and domination. We were also very relieved that our first experience with demon possession was over. That was some twenty years ago. None of us have ever encountered anything like this ordeal since.

The person with this gift does not go out looking for those needing this kind of healing, but he or she has a compassion to liberate them from demonic bondage. The gifted person yearns to see persons healed and free of demonic activity. The person will often say something like this, "Let me pray for your deliverance. Share it with me and let's get rid of the evil." Sometimes the person possessed is so relieved that she or he goes limp or is temporarily rendered unconscious.

We do not need to look for demon activity to encounter evil in all of its forms. We experience enough evil that comes from the human heart. There is the potential for good and evil in all of us. When we choose to live without God's grace, love, and power, the good within us gives way to the evil. When evil desires, greed, pride, hatred, low self-esteem, and self-centeredness cause the worst to come out of us, the good within us is suppressed and our evil inclination is released. The spiritual side of our humanity must be regenerated. Jesus' redemptive death makes this spiritual reunion with God possible.

Faith

. . . to another faith by the same Spirit . . . (1 Corinthians 12:9).

All people have some degree or level of faith. This is "general" or "common" faith. Everyone uses this basic faith in everyday living. Life requires some kind of faith.

Pistis is used in the New Testament to communicate faith in God or Christ. Faith is a means of grace that makes our redemption (or salvation) possible. It is this living faith that we trust not only in God's redemption, but also in the promises of God's grace to find forgiveness if we should sin against God or our neighbors. Without faith we cannot know God.

I strongly believe that Christians need to understand the power and authority that is behind the gift of faith in Christ's name. God energizes this kind of faith to do spiritual warfare. Perhaps like no other time in the history of the world has there been such an assault on the church of Jesus Christ by evil

A powerful book dealing with faith is Faith-Sharing *by Eddie Fox and George Morris.*

forces. There is rising interest in New Age spirituality. TV psychic programs and telephone systems pander to this curiosity. Occult practices are on the rise in the United States. Books on Satanism and witchcraft sell as fast as Christian books. Skinheads and other hate groups are definitely under the influence of demonic forces because they preach racial hatred rather than love. I believe that these and many other immoral activities are the work of demonic forces.

Those gifted with the gift of faith understand this biblical truth. The Holy Spirit empowers all believers with Christ's authority, but God energizes the basic faith of some persons in the church to a greater degree, to serve the purposes of God.

❦ How does having faith like a child help the believer deal with the world?

Giving

... the giver, in generosity ... (Romans 12:8, NRSV).

One of the best examples of a person with this gift is the widow Jesus watched making her offering (Luke 21:1-4). Despite witnessing some people make large gifts, Jesus noticed the widow and her offering of two copper coins, worth only a fraction of a penny. Bryant defines giving as "the ability to manage one's resources of income, time, energy, and skills to exceed what is considered to be a reasonable standard for giving to the church, an amount that brings joy and power to do more for future service" (page 85). This gift is measured by one's ability to give sacrificially to the needs of others, not by the amount given. Those who have this gift will often deny their own needs to help meet the needs of others.

This gift involves resources other than money such as time and skills. The results of such giving are joy, ecstasy, peace, cheerfulness, and a feeling that the person is sharing the love of God in Christ with others.

Giving is the stewardship of all believers. Persons with this *charisma* generously support and are quick to aid the church's mission. Person with the gift of giving experience joy or cheerfulness from their giving. Their joy comes from the freedom or abandonment they feel in giving to meet the needs of others.

❦ How would you describe giving in your congregation? Does your congregation give liberally or miserly? Does your church readily support new ventures in ministry?

Discuss this question: What is the biblical standard for giving?

Read aloud Bryant's definition on page 85.

Allow two or three persons to share their experiences of tithing.

Dr. Bryant writes about a golfer who was hustled. On learning that he had been swindled, he still thanked God. How do you respond to this story (page 86)?

Healings

. . . to another gifts of healing by that one Spirit . . . (1 Corinthians 12:9).

When most people think about healing, they usually think specifically about physical healing. They fail to understand that physical healing is only one of the ways God heals. As I travel around the country, teaching about the healing ministry of the church, I remind people that if we were only sick physically, we would be in good shape. Many physicians believe that some of our illnesses have a psychological root in addition to physical causes. Treatment is now offered to the whole person, including their social and religious life.

The New Testament words for healing are *iamaton* and *therapeia*, meaning "cures" or "serving to make whole or well." Paul lists healing as a *charisma* in 1 Corinthians 12:9, using *iamaton*, a plural form. The fact that the gift of healing is in the plural is evidence that healing occurs in a variety of ways.

❧ How have you witnessed healing (mental, emotional, social, etc.)?

❧ How have you experienced healing?

Our definition narrows the scope of healing as a *charisma* to a perspective not always articulated by the church. The gift of healing reminds us that God is not indifferent to human pain and suffering. Those with this gift realize that God heals in order to bring us toward transformation.

Healing is the ministry of the church. God gives some members of the church the gift of healing to continue Christ's healing ministry. Gifts, including healing, witness to Jesus Christ's continuous presence. The church will not replace the healing professions or medical sciences and technologies. Rather, the church works with these professions. Many Christians are apparently seeking both the best medical therapies and the best spiritual therapies to meet their health needs. The primary role of the church remains to offer healing, health, and salvation.

Dr. Bryant writes: "I believe the church's ability to fulfill its commission to make disciples (see Matt. 28:19-20) hinges upon healing and wholeness; the church needs a better understanding of the charismatic offering of healings" (page 90).

Persons with the gift of healing believe that the church is not to stand idle with regard to health issues. They understand that the church is a spiritual hospital where Jesus is the chief surgeon. God equips and empowers the

Express to the group that everyone needs some kind of healing: physical, emotional, spiritual, relational.

Allow time for the group to discuss this question: How is salvation a spiritual journey toward health and wholeness?

What is the difference between a healing and a cure?

Ask the group how they feel and think about this claim.

Ask the group to respond to this summary of the three-fold purpose of the healing ministry of the church:
1. To help one another experience spiritual reunion (conversion) with God through Jesus Christ.
2. To help one another maintain a harmonious balance in each human being's total life dimensions: spirit, body, mind (emotions), and relationships.
3. To help one another restore or repair the life dimensions: spirit, body, mind, and relationships.

People often ask, "Who are the elders of the church we are to have pray and anoint us?" Churches have different traditions, and an elder may be a consecrated lay person or an ordained person. Ask the group to consider this statement: Since anointing with oil is not a sacrament among Protestants, anyone who has oversight for a group may serve as an elder.

church of Jesus Christ with *charismata* to minister to all of the diverse needs of people.

True healers do not try to figure out why some persons are healed and some are not. They believe that sickness can happen to anyone at any time, for a variety of reasons. A person can have a right relationship with God and neighbor and still not be well in body and mind. A person can have a healthy body and mind and still be ill spiritually. Healers believe that health and wholeness are life-time processes. Gifted persons emphasize that the sick person is to pray first and also to use common sense. The person seeking healing must be open to healing therapy through every means that God provides, including health care professionals.

Persons with the gift of healing are keenly aware of the need to bring healing and wholeness to people. They realize that they are God's instruments of healing and that God is the cure-giver (or healer). Most persons with this gift rarely hold healing crusades with fanfare and personalized billing. The reason is simple. They do not desire to draw attention to themselves. They believe that healing is best understood within the context of Christian community where faith in the healing ministry can be fostered and grow, bringing healing to the whole church.

James 5:14-20 strongly suggests that the church think of its mission as a healing community. Sick people are encouraged to take the initiative to call on the elders of the church so the elders may pray over them, anoint them with oil, and lay hands upon them. Perhaps the early church thought of healing as a sacramental act. The healing act seems to depend on the gift of faith on the part of the elders, not upon the individuals seeking healing. This lesson is one we continue to learn. Anointing with oil serves several purposes. It was a medical remedy used in that day. Oil serves as a symbol of God's healing presence. Oil helps persons release their faith or to open themselves to the healing power of the Holy Spirit. Anointing with oil by an elder is a gesture of love, compassion, and physical presence toward the sick person. In addition to healing the sick person, God also offers forgiveness to the person being restored to health.

Persons gifted as healers believe that healing and evangelism are connected to church growth. The Bible reveals that large numbers of people turn to God for salvation when authentic healing and miracles occur. Those who witnessed the powerful demonstrations of miracles and healing by Philip the evangelist believed in Christ and were baptized into the kingdom of God (Acts 8:6-12). Healing demonstrates God's presence, compassion, and love toward suffering humanity.

❧ Write your needs for healing in these areas:
Body

Mind

Feelings

Relations

Spirit

Work

❧ How does your congregation offer healing in the areas listed above?

Helps

. . . third teachers, then workers of miracles, also those having gifts of healing, those able to help others . . . (1 Corinthians 12:28).

The Greek word for helps comes from *antilempsis*, which means "to aid and assist another in need." This word is found only once in the New Testament (1 Cor. 12:28).

No sense of charity is implied in this gift. The real motivation of the gift is the potential for building relationships in the body of Christ. Those having the gift of helps value the intimate relationships that are often established through the experience of Christian giving and receiving. Investing their ministry-gift in the lives of others establishes lifelong relationships.

The gift of helps is the unique capacity that God endows some members of the body of Christ to increase the proficiency of grace-gifts of other members in the body. Without persons with the gift of helps, we could not minister in the body of Christ.

God bestows the gift of helps on many people because the needs within the body of Christ are so great. These persons are priceless within the life of the church. Those who realize that they possess this gift offer their time, skills, energy, and talents to save the church money, energy, and other resources. Their help is measured by the lives they touch and the friendships they foster. Bryant's belief that this gift is abundant in the church should not surprise anyone.

❧ Name one person with the gift of helps who has touched your life. How has that person helped you?

Note the distinction Bryant makes between helps and service. One deals with needs of persons and the other focuses on the worship of God.

Hospitality

Share with God's people who are in need. Practice hospitality (Romans 12:13).

Individuals with the gift of hospitality have a special love or fondness toward strangers. They invite strangers (or those outside their common circle) into their homes and freely give special attention in caring for their needs and comfort. The Greek word for hospitality is *philonexia*, which means "love or fondness of strangers."

Jerry and Ann Horner truly have the gift of hospitality. I have known the Horners since 1974, and I cannot remember visiting their home when they did not welcome some stranger as a guest in their home. When I first met the Horners, Jerry invited my family of eight persons to their temporary home in a small apartment while their home was being repaired after a tornado. They did not know us. They are simply remarkable Christian people who have a genuine love for strangers. They consider the need and comfort of the strangers above their own. Their home is offered for the service and glory of God. The Horners often go beyond the second and third mile to show or manifest Christ's love to the concerns of strangers.

Those who experience persons with the gift of hospitality feel valued. There is a warm attraction that draws persons to those with the gift of hospitality. They have the ability to make others feel welcome and give attention to the strangers' needs and desires. They are people-centered and not program or group-centered. Those individuals experience joy in meeting strangers and do not feel threatened by their presence.

Those with the gift of hospitality enable the ministry of the church to invite and receive strangers, making them feel welcome and thereby bringing new vitality and spiritual health to the church. Persons with this gift offer a pleasant or sustaining environment where persons are given a generous and cordial welcome (Rom. 12:13; 1 Tim. 5:10; 1 Pet. 4:9). Paul stresses that Christians should practice hospitality, which "means to tend to the welfare or well-being of others."

Sometimes people confuse hospitality and evangelism. Dr. Bryant points out that one with the gift of hospitality sees Christ in the stranger (Matt. 25:35) whereas the evangelist visualizes the stranger in Christ (Acts 8:26-40). The church in North America desperately needs to benefit from this gift to balance out the serious decline taking place in our churches. Too many churches fail to reach out to people and make them feel welcome and needed. We need to rediscover the gift of hospitality, to identify, and to make opportunities for those with this gift to serve.

❧ On a scale from one to ten, with one being equivalent to a security gate across your congregation's doors and ten equivalent to a welcoming committee on the street offering valet parking, how would you rank your church's gift of hospitality?

Encourage the group to talk about hospitality as critical to the ministry of the church. The way we welcome people into our churches speaks loudly about our understanding of God's love. All churches must have a warm heart and a personal touch to draw in people rather than push them out or neglect them.

Most churches disregard this vital ministry altogether. Encourage members of the group to challenge their churches to rediscover this gift.

Humor

A cheerful heart is good medicine, but a crushed spirit dries up the bones.
(Proverbs 17:22)

The Rev. Gregg Parris, Dr. Allen Coppedge, and I served as leaders for the 16th Annual United Methodist Conference on the Holy Spirit. After hearing Gregg Parris preach three messages, I realized that he has the gifts of preaching and humor. He used humor to get the attention of the audience. His humor helped to put people at ease.

Humor makes difficult subject matters less threatening and helps to release tension or to bring peace within people. Humor enables people to hear a message they probably would not hear in any other context. This gift offers a different perspective on a topic and provides another way to communicate ideas, concepts, biblical truths.

Those gifted with humor always tell jokes in good taste to bring healing and wholeness in people. They never stereotype people. Humor is never used to put down racial, ethnic, cultural differences, or the physical features of people.

Those with the gift of humor combine faith, facts, and fun in a religious context and at the same time glorify God. Humor is often a sacred opportunity to use emotions to transform harsh realities into manageable means of faith living. "[One] who laughs well also lives well" (page 98).

❦ Some people think of Christianity as a dour, dry, dull religion. How can the gift of humor help people recognize the abundant joy that is life in Christ?

Intercessory Prayer

Therefore he is able to save completely those who come to God
through him, because he always lives to intercede for them.
(Hebrews 7:25)

The Greek word for intercessory prayer is *enteuxis* and means "petition," a "bringing together," or "intervention on another's behalf." We often forget that Jesus Christ intercedes for those who turn to God for salvation. The risen Christ is our permanent and continuous intercessor before God to plead our case or to seek our protection (John 17:15-26; Heb. 7:25). The Holy Spirit also makes intercession for us when we do not know how to pray (Rom. 8:26-27).

Intercession is the extraordinary ability to know when, how, and for whom or what to pray. Persons with this gift have a tremendous capacity and desire to pray for extended periods of time on a regular basis on behalf of others. Intercessors experience success in seeing specific answers to their prayers. They persevere in prayer until, by faith, something happens. The gift

Ask the group to name biblical characters or persons within the church who use the gift of humor in their ministry. What lessons do they teach us about the value and place of humor within the life of the church?

Discuss Bryant's statement about humor with the group: "[One] who laughs well also lives well."

Have any participants discovered that they have this gift? Have them share some of their experiences. Do others in the study affirm the gift?

Give a brief summary of the different forms of prayer (prayers of thanksgiving, confession, adoration, etc.).

Ask participants to write a definition of intercessory prayer in the margin. Invite them to share the different forms of prayer they use. Then, ask them to underline the form of prayer that is the most meaningful to them.

of intercessory prayer is different from the general role of praying that is common to every believer. Those without the gift of intercession do not have the power to persist in prayer until something happens. Those with the gift of intercession have a dynamic dimension that sets them apart from others without the gift. Once they believe that their praying has fulfilled its purpose, they release it to God. They believe that what they are praying for is already a reality. Intercessors see their prayer as ministry to the body of Christ.

Bryant points out that intercessors often have a prayer language. The unknown language helps their intercession because they do not always know why or what to pray. The prayer language frees the mind to focus on the person or situation, and it empowers persons to pray for long periods of time without the feeling of fatigue or confusion. At the conclusion of such intercession, there is always an overwhelming sense of peaceful completion. Intercession is hard work and requires the energizing power of the Holy Spirit. Some intercessors pray for long hours without sleep or food. Fasting often accompanies their intercession. Praying and fasting are normal parts of their spiritual disciplines.

Billy Graham has always recognized the importance of intercessory prayer. Intercessors pray for his crusades months and years in advance. Before the Rev. Ezekiel Guti (see page 39) conducts revivals or hold pastors' conferences or does any form of ministry, his prayer ministry joins in intercession before and during these events.

More Christian churches are rediscovering this vital gift, and many are beginning to use its powerful effect to strengthen and to revitalize the local church. Every church should have intercessors praying for the church throughout the week.

Before I became part of The Upper Room, I was encouraged by Dr. Terry Teykl to establish prayer partners for this new ministry. I recognized this as wisdom from the Lord. I began to ask people to become a part of my prayer ministry. Today, over eighty persons pray for my ministry. My schedule is sent to each of them. They know where I will be ministering and the specific kind of event. I also pray for them, their families, and their ministries.

❧ When have you joined in intercessory prayers? Did you feel challenged, comfortable, hopeful, disappointed, or beat?

Interpretation

> . . . and to still another the interpretation of tongues (1 Corinthians. 12:10).

The Greek word for "interpretation" is *diermeneuo*, meaning "to make clear" or "to expound on a meaning for understanding." Interpretation is "the

Have the participants form groups of two. Invite them to share why it is important to the health and growth of the church for persons to operate in their particular gifts and callings.

Have a person read aloud the text from page 103. Emphasize the point that the presence of this gift is necessary if the gift of tongues is to edify the church.

extraordinary ability to hear, comprehend, and translate spiritual messages given by others in unknown languages or to clarify spiritual messages from one who speaks in a known language, not known by the interpreters" (page 103).

The gift of interpretation, or more accurately named the gift of interpretation of tongues, validates the gift of tongues. Without the gift of interpretation, the tongues have no value or benefit to the body of Christ. When people are open to the guidance of the Holy Spirit, both gifts are present for the edification of the body of Christ.

Some persons consider tongues and interpretation as a hyphenated gift (tongues-interpretation). They believe it is unusual for a person to have the gift of interpretation without the accompanying gift of tongues. Often one person brings a message in tongues and another interprets. In some cases, the same person brings the message in a language and also gives the interpretation. The body of Christ is to judge the message and the interpretation, but not the gifted persons. In most cases the language given is unknown to both the gifted person and those hearing the message. However, at times the message in tongues may be in a language known to someone in the gathered body. The hearers understand the language because it is in their own tongue.

Dr. Bryant's concern for the gift of interpretation needs emphasis. The gospel of God's love has been distorted so that the church is divided and often powerless. Only sound interpretation can deliver us from this evil. God has given this spiritual gift of interpretation for this purpose (see page 104).

Help the members understand that the tongues, like other gifts, are intended to promote wholeness and healing. Read Bryant's comments on pages 103–104. Ask participants what they think about this claim.

Jesus Christ had the ability to interpret God's love and grace in such a way that those who heard him turned to God for life and faith. The gift of interpretation is given to balance the gift of tongues. Remember that whatever does not help or strengthen the church has no real value. Paul addressed the abuse of the gift of tongues in Corinth and warned the people to be wise so that the gifts would not contradict the freedom of the gospel. We are to use the gifts only when they guarantee effective results for the edification and growth of the church.

❧ Paul stressed that love should accompany the gift of tongues and of interpretation. The contemporary church should practice this principle.

In what way is God calling this gift within you?

Knowledge

. . . to another the message of knowledge by means of the same Spirit. . . .
(*1 Corinthians 12:8*)

The gift of knowledge is a special ability God gives to some individuals to discover divine truth about God's grace expressed through Christ's redemptive work. The Greek word for this gift is *gnosis*, discovering universal and timeless truths and facts relating to God's will and the mission of the church, or of God's reign.

Have a person read aloud this definition of the gift of knowledge, then ask this question: How does knowledge differ from discernment?

Persons with knowledge have the ability to comprehend a truth or fact as God sees it. God gives all believers general knowledge, imparted by the Holy Spirit. The Holy Spirit gives knowledge as to who Christ is, their relationship to him, and how to relate Christ in their daily life, and to the world. Persons with this gift are able to perceive the differences between religion and science, the spiritual and the material, and the historical biblical message and the modern mind, according to Bryant (page 106).

Some individuals confuse the gifts of knowledge with the gift of discernment. They are not the same. Bryant notes that knowledge can be measured by reason, logic, and authority given by God. Those with the gift of knowledge have a calm assurance that they know what they know is of divine truth. They can communicate these truths about God. They have the ability to make God's Word come alive for others.

It is important not to seek knowledge from just anyone. Know your source. The authentic gift of knowledge is given in order that the body of Christ may more effectively mediate the grace of Christ to human needs.

♦ Name the person who has most fluently taught you about God. Offer prayers of thanks for that person.

Leadership

"... if it is leadership ... govern diligently" (Romans 12:8).

Discuss why Bryant believes that leaders are poor followers. How do they compensate for this?

A person gifted in leadership has the ability to guide others to fulfill the mission of the church of Jesus Christ. Leadership comes from the Greek word *proistemi*, meaning "to lead, guide, or direct." *Proistemi* suggests the role of a sailor standing on the bow of a ship to point out directions and to guide the ship around dangers.

People with this gift do not force others to use their gifts for the well being of the kingdom. They usually have a gentle way of getting people to work together for the common good. They affirm the gifts of others and motivate them to use their gifts to accomplish God's will and purpose for the building of the kingdom.

Stress what Bryant writes about leadership. Although the leaders have unique abilities and gifts, churches must provide many opportunities for them to receive the training they need to develop into the leaders God is calling them to become.

Usually the gift of faith accompanies the gift of leadership. The leader's confidence in the gifts and graces of others to get the task done helps to motivate others to give their best to God's purpose for the church. Gifted leaders develop skills of communication for self-motivation. Those in leadership are not good followers because of their strong inclination to lead. Some interpret their strong desire to lead as being self-centeredness. Leaders are not egocentric; they strive to do nothing to create disunity or to work against the goals of the church. They are able to follow others, but will look for opportunities to offer leadership because, Dr. Bryant reasons, they are more visionary than practical and more futuristic than contemporary. People follow gifted leaders primarily because they demonstrate the virtues of Christ.

The gift of leadership is necessary to set goals in accordance to the will and purposes of God within the life of the church. These goals must be communicated so that others will offer their service and work for the good of the whole body of Christ.

❧ Who shows the gifts of leadership for your congregation? How can you support the leaders?

Martyrdom

If I give all I possess to the poor and surrender my body to the flames, but have not love, I gain nothing (1 Corinthians 13:3).

The gift of martyrdom is perhaps more widespread than we often think. I appreciate Dr. Bryant's broader understanding of the gift of martyrdom. Martyrdom is "the extraordinary ability to stand firm on divinely inspired convictions and divinely directed ministries without equivocation or self-aggrandizement" (page 110-11). Perhaps the Christians from the old Soviet Union and those who lived in other nations that have tried to eliminate Christianity can teach those of us who live in the United States about martyrdom.

The practice of spiritual disciplines undergirds this gift, particular that of prayer and fasting. Without prayer, our gifts lack the energizing power our gifts require.

Remind the group that all of the gifts are secondary in the Christian life to agape love being active in one's life. Without God's charismatic (energizing) love working in us, we cannot produce any positive results for growth and health in the body of Christ.

❧ How do you respond to stories about Christian martyrs?

❧ How do you respond to those who maintain their Christian convictions despite persecution?

Mercy

Blessed are the merciful, for they will be shown mercy (Matthew 5:7).

Just as all Christians have a measure of faith, they also have a measure of mercy. Showing mercy is a by-product of the Spirit working in the life of the Christian. Jesus placed acts of compassion and mercy as a high priority of his own life and ministry. He understood that God's call upon his life was one of compassion and mercy (Luke 4:18-21). Jesus also calls his followers to continue his ministry of compassion in the world to those considered "the least" (Matt. 25:42-45).

Ask participants to identify the "untouchables" in our culture. Write this list on newsprint or a chalkboard.

Allow time for the group to discuss how God is calling the church to offer acts of love and compassion to those who are poor, suffering, and disenfranchised.

The aim of this gift is to relieve the suffering of distress, pain, and discomfort of those in the body of Christ. They have a special capacity to feel and act upon the pain and suffering of others as an expression of Christ's compassion for the church and the world (John 3:16; 2 Cor. 5:19).

Those with this gift reflect the compassion and love of Christ for those who are broken and suffering. Their ministry is usually to one person at a time. They do not discriminate. Their mission is to eliminate as much suffering and pain as possible. They believe that God cares about those who are poor, mentally and physically challenged, and marginalized.

They strive to communicate that God is not indifferent to pain and sufferings. They demonstrate divine love, not just human love.

Most persons who have the gift of mercy are powerful witnesses of Jesus Christ and would not do anything to hurt the body of Christ. They realize that they are blessed by their acts of compassion and love and open their lives to the hurting and suffering because they can do nothing less. They believe that they are blessed because their gift empowers them to identify with the suffering (Matt. 5:7). Their acts of mercy bring joy and relief to those being helped when they do it in a spirit of cheerfulness (Rom. 12:8).

This gift is often used in completely secular settings, without the benefits of the resources of the church. Like Bryant, I believe that the gifts works best within the context of the church. Bryant makes this keen observation: "No gift is designed to work exclusively outside the body of Christ. Yet, many gifts are forced to operate in secular situations almost exclusively because of the church's ignorance or disinterest. So, when the church does not provide opportunities for certain gifts to be used within, the gifted with mercy can serve the body well as catalysts who call the church's attention to opportunities to relieve the suffering and debilitating conditions of others outside" (page 116).

Miracles

> . . . to another miraculous powers . . . (1 Cointhians 12:10).

Many people believe that miracles passed away with the apostolic age. Some of those persons preach in our pulpits, teach in our schools, and translate the Bible. They belong to your church and my church. Some of them are our mothers, fathers, sisters, brothers, and neighbors. Yet, miracles still happen with great regularity! God still gives some people the ability to do powerful works in Christ's name.

What is a miracle? A miracle represents "powerful operations" or "powerful works." Miracles relate to many of the other gifts, but we do not fully understand how. We know that this gift enhances or elevates the other gifts to a dimension that causes a change in nature or the natural laws from time to time to serve the will and purpose of God. This power or energy does not come from natural laws or natural phenomena.

Persons with the gift of miracles often do not know when this gift is going to be accomplished. They respond to an inner prompting of the Holy

Close this section by reading aloud this statement by Bryant on page 116. Ask them what they feel and think about this claim.

State that perhaps the gifts of healing and miracles are the best known of all of the gifts. Yet, they are generally misunderstood by many people.

Allow time for persons to tell about miracles they have experienced.

Spirit to meet a specific need. They are often surprised when the powerful manifestation of energies in response to a prompted need.

Because of the authentic nature of miracles, people find it difficult to comprehend how human beings could possess such an awesome ability or giftedness that could work outside the natural laws. Yet, both the Old and New Testaments record numerous miracles God wrought through human instruments.

I have witnessed miracles of healing in the many different dimensions of life. I have experienced the miracle of answered prayers. I have experienced signs from God about my journey in faith. In 1974 I left a teaching career to enter an evangelistic ministry and was led to Oral Roberts University. Even as we drove to visit the university, my wife and I received signs and answers to our prayers that affirmed our decisions. We looked for those answers. For example, our first stop from Newark, Delaware, to Tulsa, Oklahoma, was in my hometown of Roanoke, Virginia. Mother asked if my brother Jimmy had told us about the healing of his stomach ulcer after my wife Gloria and I prayed for him and laid hands on him. We had not heard, but this was a sign of encouragement. We then drove to Knoxville, Tennessee, where I asked about the charismatic community. I learned about Dr. Edward Eyring, who was then a Catholic charismatic. Ed and Mary Jane and their five children gave us (my wife, me, and our six children) hospitality in their home. While eating with the Eyrings, I learned that Ed had a lot of pain in his back and in the joints of his fingers. Gloria and I told Ed that we believed in God's healing power and would like to pray for his healing. We prayed together and God's healing power found expression in Ed's body. The pain was instantly gone.

Other events happened on that trip in response to our prayers. Gloria and I had prayed about whether I was being led to a new vocation. All that happened on that trip to Oklahoma and back to Delaware confirmed God's new direction for us as Gloria and I both learned about our spiritual gifts.

Perhaps more people do not experience miracles today because they do not want to see miracles.

❧ Do you expect to witness miracles?

Missionary

Therefore go and make disciples of all nations . . . (Matthew 28:19).

Part of my thinking about this gift is shaped by the book *Faith-Sharing* by Eddie Fox and George Morris. They insist that our understanding of mission comes from God, who is a missionary God. God initiates the relationship with humankind. God is the seeker. Not only is God a seeking God, but a sending God. Therefore, God is empowering and challenging the church to become an instrument that seeks and sends. God comes into the broken order of our lives to be in a relationship with us. God's love will not let us go.

We are in mission because we serve a God who is in love with us, who will not let us go, and who wants the whole world to know about that love. Do

Close this study of this gift by praising God for the blessings of gifts.

Invite someone to read aloud the definition of this gift. Ask if they know anyone with this gift. List the locations of these missionaries. What special qualities do they seem to have? Ask if any members of the group have been resisting this call to ministry? If so, take a few moments to pray with him or her, inviting the Holy Spirit's power and grace to help the person be able to answer this call to ministry. Show your love and give encouragement.

not confuse mission with witnessing. Every Christian is called to witness, but not everyone has the calling of a missionary. God calls certain members of the body of Christ to serve as missionaries to go outside their culture to spread the good news of the gospel. Persons with this gift "have an extraordinary ability to cross over the boundaries of races, color, creed, language, geography, culture, and subcultures to serve the physical, psychological, social, and spiritual needs of neglected peoples" (page 119).

Perhaps many ethnic persons have not seen themselves gifted with this gift because doors were closed to them and they have been the target of evangelization. Yet, I believe that the Holy Spirit is beginning to do a new thing where they will recognize God's call to the missionary gift. They will be our future missionaries. Peoples and cultures who have negative views of ethnic people will become the recipients of a new breed of missionaries. They will bring a new understanding, experience, and witness to the gospel of salvation and liberation.

❧ How would your church or community respond if someone came as a missionary to the community?

Fox and Morris remind us that we do not have missions, but we are in mission with a loving God who is constantly seeking and sending the church to reach out to all of humanity with God's salvation.

Missionaries come from all walks of life. Some may be medical specialists (relating to humans beings and animals), lawyers, economists, industrial engineers, teachers of basic human skills, or agronomists. They may be foresters, carpenters, plumbers, electricians, civil engineers, or road builders.

What makes these gifted persons special is the way the Holy Spirit enables them to cross cultural barriers and to feel at peace in very different settings with new peoples and new cultures. Their warm and contagious personalities radiate the love of Christ. Persons with this gift have a passionate desire and dream to fulfill Christ's mandate to take the gospel to all the world. They actually see the world won for Christ. Their vision and their destiny is to help spread the gospel where it has not yet been heard or where the gospel is severely restricted. The authentic missionary must be affirmed and supported with our prayers and financial support. As Christians, we must pray for the salvation of the whole world.

Pastor

. . . and some to be pastors and teachers . . . (Ephesians 4:11).

Point out that the New Testament model of pastor is also that of a gifted teacher. This is a mixed gift of pastor-teacher. Pastors must be able teachers to rightly interpret the revelations of the Word of God and to foster spiritual growth and maturity in the body of Christ.

A shepherd caring for the sheep is the common image of the authentic pastor. The pastor is a person God calls out to shepherd and care for the spiritual and physical needs of a group of people. The Greek word for "pastor" is *poimen*, meaning "shepherd." The word means "to protect," "to oversee," "to care for," "to assemble," and "to feed." Pastoring as a gift is evident when it brings shepherding, heals wounds, maintains community, helps persons discover their gifts, provides opportunities for the use of gifts, engages in mission, proclaims the good news, and engages in Bible study and the other spiritual disciplines.

The authentic pastor is quick to recognize that his or her ministry involves the entire body. The authentic pastor can shoulder concerns for the multiple needs of many people while he or she helps them grow spiritually. Pastors are often able teachers, though this is not true of each pastor. Sometimes the gift of teaching stands alone as a single gift (Eph. 4:11). I strongly believe that the gift of the pastor must be affirmed by the body of Christ. The gift is valid whether the person seeks ordination or not. There are many opportunities for the use of the gift without following the track of ordination. Small groups such as shepherding groups, house groups, prayer groups, and cell groups, when functioning properly encouraging members into mutual caring dynamics, are using the gift of the pastor.

Pastoral leaders must attend to the needs of the congregation. They must look for others in the congregation with the gift of pastoring to help them discover, develop, and use this gift to care for others. When the health and growth of a congregation is lacking, look first to determine whether the pastor-member ratio is out of balance. Offset this vital imbalance to restore the health and growth of the church.

❦ Have you discovered yourself serving as pastor to a small group such as one at work or in Sunday school?

Prayer-Praise Language

... to another the ability to speak in different kinds of tongues ... (1 Cointhians 12:10).

The prayer and praise language of the Christian is one of the most misunderstood and divisive of the body of Christ. The confusion centered around this gift has been with the Christian church from the start. One who prays in the prayer-praise language is speaking to God (1 Cor. 14:2). The prayer language is beyond human comprehension because it is a supernatural utterance given to the speaker by the Holy Spirit. It has nothing to do with linguistic ability or intellectual capacity. The person does the speaking, but the Holy Spirit gives the utterance. Praying in tongues is always under our control, but we need the language of the Spirit of God.

Praying in a prayer language is something that we do with the help of the Holy Spirit. The Spirit's involvement in private prayer tongues is in the giving of the words. Because this is an act of a person's will, one with the gift can use prayer tongues anytime. The Spirit does not take the person over as

The gift of tongues is greatly misunderstood. Sometimes this gift is abused. What have you been taught in church about prayer language? What have you learned from other sources about such language?

some believe. The person praying is always fully conscious and is aware of what is going on.

Prayer tongues are only beneficial to the one praying with the Spirit (verse 3). The person speaking in the prayer language is edified, strengthened, and helped (verse 4). Prayer tongues enable the person to express deep inward yearnings to God at times when the mind or intellect are unfruitful. There are times when words fail to communicate the deep true feelings within us that we desire to speak to God. There are times when our hearts are so filled with praise, adoration, and thanksgiving to God that our language cannot communicate, but our prayer tongues enable us to speak then to God.

I strongly believe that tongues release or liberate the Spirit of God within us to bring healing and wholeness for the body, mind, and spirit. Perhaps the tongues bring balance or healing within us. Persons I know who try to describe the value of tongues suggest therapeutic benefits of prayer tongues in energizing the mind, emotions, human spirit, and body. They often say that they experience a sense of inward joy or spiritual refreshment.

Speaking in tongues is not unique to Christianity. It has a long history among some of the pagan religions and cultic practices. The confusion of its practices extends from that time to the present, not because of its psychological or social value but because of its misunderstandings and abuses. Paul's teaching on this gift is to address some of the abuses he discusses in chapters twelve through fourteen of 1 Corinthians.

Prayer tongues are strictly for individual and private prayer. The tongues do not comply to any formulas or patterns. Each person's prayer-praise language is distinctly individual. When and how persons use the gift also varies. The languages or utterances vary from prayer to prayer or from praise to praise. Persons using the gift most often begin praying in their own language and then move into their prayer language. Prayer tongues enable us to overcome the language restriction between God and ourselves. Tongues become the means of grace of bridging the language (communication) gap.

The two basic understandings of prayer tongues identify tongues as either for individual benefit or for the benefit of the whole church. Paul wants everyone to have the prayer language, but in 1 Corinthians 14 Paul makes clear that he would rather people understand clearly God's purpose. Paul believed that our concern should always be to help and edify the community of faith above ourselves. Christians should seek those which edify and build up the church (verse 12).

Much emphasis has been placed on this gift, perhaps to the detriment of all believers. Prayer-language offers skeptics the opportunity to deny the truth of Jesus Christ. Not all Christians pray aloud, but they are authentic Christians and have a meaningful prayer life. We should emphasize the Spirit's power in producing new life in us, rather than emphasizing only one manifestation of the Spirit's presence and power.

The answer to question four on the true/false quiz is false. Neither the gift of tongues nor any of the gifts is the authentic sign of the baptism of the

Not everyone has the gift of tongues given to edify the body. In Romans 8 Paul seems to suggest that everyone has the ability to pray in prayer tongues for when we do not know how to pray the Spirit helps us (Rom. 8:26-27).

Much love is required with tongues because of confusion and abuse centered around it. Pray that God will help the church to provide opportunities for all of the gifts to be used for the edification and growth of the body.

Holy Spirit. The only authentic sign of the presence of the Spirit in the life of the Christian is love (agape). And along with love comes obedience. If either of them is missing, so is the Spirit of God. The fruit of the Spirit defines the Spirit's presence, the Christ-like character of the believer. The gift of the Spirit defines the ministry of the believer. The gifts and the fruit of the Spirit come as gifts from God.

Tongues are not to be forbidden or limited either in corporate worship or during individual prayer. Tongues remain under the control of the person. I believe that some people do not speak in tongues because they do not want to lose control. Giving up control for some of us is interpreted as a sign of weakness. Yielding the most unruly part of us (the tongue) to the Spirit, in my estimation, is a most wise decision. Praying in the power of the Spirit (using prayer-praise tongues) is the most perfect way to pray, but it is not the only way to pray. I believe that the new spiritual life we have in Christ requires a new way to communicate with God, in the Spirit. Prayer-praise form of praying is not common to everyone, therefore, not everyone uses it.

Jot responses to the following questions raised by Dr. Bryant (pages 127–128) about *glossalalia*:

❦ Does the gift increase one's patience and love toward others?

❦ Does the gift leave one feeling closer to Christ?

❦ Does the gift cause one to look up, straight across, or down to others?

❦ Does its use cause one to feel superior or extra special in God's family.

❦ Do some ever use it as a shorthand or an easy way of praying?

❦ Does one feel addicted to its use, that is, one cannot pray without it?

❦ Does he or she feel it is necessary to tell everyone about the gift?

❦ Can one be away from others who use it aloud without having great discomfort?

❦ Is there shame or timidity associated with its use?

❦ Is there a guilt feeling over its use or lack of use?

Prophecy

We have gifts that differ according to the grace given us: prophecy in proportion to faith" (Roman 12:6, NSRV).

Have a person read aloud the definition of prophecy on page 129.

Participants may need to discuss differences between biblical prophets and prophecy and contemporary understandings of fortune telling or reading the future.

The Greek word for "prophecy" is *propheteia* or "revealing, manifesting, showing forth, making known, divulging, speaking out, or announcing vital information necessary for spiritual living and development." Dr. Bryant more broadly defines this *charisma* as "the extraordinary ability to link biblical truths with God's will for today's living and to be an instrument for revealing or interpreting previous or current messages from God for righteous and just living in today's world" (page 129).

People today think of prophecy as predicting the future. Authentic prophecy deals more with present situations, conditions, and events. Biblical prophets spoke God's messages with regard to current situations concerning God's relationship with humanity. That pattern holds true today. God's message may be that of correction, encouragement, guidance, or judgment. Serving as a prophet is a very difficult and thankless ministry. Most prophets suffer some kind of hardship. They are often misunderstood because they present unpopular messages that demand a spiritual or moral response.

Those with the gift of prophecy have a keen perspective of God's kingdom and righteousness, encompassing all aspects of life, not just the spiritual. The prophetic message is not taken lightly. The prophet urgently calls for a response from listeners. Prophets often appear to be impatient or restless. They are result driven rather than process-oriented. They may act out or illustrate their message in some unconventional visual methods.

❧ Think about these biblical prophets: Nathan, Amos, Micah, Hosea. What messages do you identify with them?

❧ Name one person whom you feel has the gift of prophecy. What message does that person bring?

Service

There are different kinds of service, but the same Lord (1 Corinthians 12:5).

Tell the students that God gives talents and spiritual endowments to equip each individual to serve others in Christ's name.

In a church I served, the phrase "we are all ministers" was printed on the Sunday bulletin. Those words reminded us that every baptized person is a minister in the body of Christ. Christ calls every believer to participate in his mission and ministry. All Christians are ministers in the body of Christ, the priesthood of all believers. We serve in Christ's name.

The Greek word for this gift is *diakonia* or servant. Jesus told his disciples that he did not come to be served, but to serve. Meeting the unmet needs of individuals or institutions is a godly act that honors God. Persons with this gift model their service after that of Jesus Christ.

The gift of service is task-oriented, following the patterns of Matthew 25. No need is too small and no needy person is beyond their attention or concern.

The gift of service is not the same as the gifts of helps or mercy. People with the gift of service are usually multi-talented with a broad range of abilities. When needs arise, they are the first to serve. They are often the quiet ones who take care of all the mundane tasks. They experience God in everything they do.

When this gift is lacking in the church, the body of Christ suffers. Every Christian has received some gift or gifts to serve the body in whatever capacity the Spirit deems is necessary for the well being of the church.

Give persons a chance to share any new insights or concerns.

❧ How have you experienced the gift of service?

Singleness

I would like you to be free from concern. One who is unmarried is concerned about the Lord's affairs—how he can please the Lord. . . .
(1 Corinthians 7:32-33)

Ask for a volunteer to read from page 135 of Bryant's book. Any aspect of sexuality combined with faith is often a difficult topic for many people to discuss. How can an unmarried person serve God and the church differently than a married person? What are the benefits of married Christians serving the body of Christ?

Paul says that singleness is a gift given by God to certain persons. Paul reasons that this gift offers time for special service to mission and ministry. Most people do not have this gift. Singleness as a gift is a religious commitment that frees persons to devote themselves fully to the service of God.

The Greek word for "singleness" is *agamos*, which means "unmarried," "unbound," "unattached." Singleness "is the extraordinary ability to offer God and the church a life unbound by marriage and free of sexual frustrations and social attachments so that one may spend the time and energy necessary for building up the chruch" (page 135). Often churches burden single people with expectations concerning marriage. Churches also tend to plan family-oriented programs and to ignore the needs of single persons. As you think about the gift of singleness, take time to reflect on the place of single persons in your congregation.

Our culture and the church have imposed guilt upon persons who receive the call to singleness. Most persons who remain single are stigmatized or slandered for being sexually promiscuous. Persons with this gift live highly successful and victorious lives serving God. They are very sociable, enjoy being around people, and have wholesome relationships with all people. Their spirituality allows them to focus their interests and energies on service to the body of Christ. They are aware of their sexuality, but they have a special spiritual power to keep their sexuality under control. I agree with Bryant that persons truly called to this gift will not be overcome with sexual frustration. With this gift comes an anointing of the Holy Spirit that gives the person God's power and grace to keep the sexual drive under their control.

Earlier I stated that the gifts are not given to us fully developed. We should also recognize that we ought not settle for just anything to be an authentic gift without devoting enough time and experience for confirmation from God. We often get into situations, such as marriage and childbearing, without knowing God had other plans for us. Our loving God provides healing grace through forgiveness. The opportunity to fulfill our divine destiny will come. We are to simply wait!

Spirit-Music

> *Sing to the LORD a new song; sing to the LORD, all the earth. Sing to the LORD, praise his name; proclaim his salvation day after day (Psalm 96: 1-2).*

Many people testify that they became aware of their musical ability or gift after their baptism in the Holy Spirit. Some of those persons are famous personalities in the gospel music industry today. Before this spiritual awakening, they had no prior knowledge of any musical ability. Some had very little or no basic musical training or aptitude for music. Although my wife, Gloria, is a college trained musician, she has the gift of Spirit-music. The music she composes has an anointing upon it and lifts the spirit. The description of her music is typical of all Spirit-music.

God gives special creative gifts to some members of the church to create inspirational music, poems, and songs to help God's people to give authentic worship. This gift enables others to enter into a higher level of experience in worship. It aids us to worship God with our whole self. It also removes barriers to grace, allowing our true feelings and emotions to be liberated so that our whole selves experience communion with God.

Stress that the work of grace of the Spirit empowers all believers to keep their sexuality in check. The charismatic life of the believer is a life of victory in all aspects of life. The difference is that those with the gift of singleness are totally complete as persons in the unmarried state.

See if there are such gifted persons in this group. Give them the opportunity to express this gift. They might design a worship experience to begin or close one of the sessions.

Read Bryant's definition of this gift on page 139, and ask the members what they think about this meaning.

Paul gives instruction for the worship services of the early church. "Speak to one another with psalms, hymns, and spiritual songs. Sing and make music in your hearts to the Lord, always giving thanks to God the Father for everything, in the name of the Lord Jesus Christ" (Eph. 5:19; 1 Cor. 14:15).

❧ What song do you identify with this study of the gifts of the Spirit? What song expresses your faith?

Suffering

Dear friends, do not be surprised at the painful trial you are suffering, as though something strange were happening to you. But rejoice that you participate in the sufferings of Christ, so that you may be overjoyed when his glory is revealed. . . . However, if you suffer as a Christian, do not be ashamed, but praise God that you bear that name"(1 Peter 4:12-13,16).

The word suffering comes from the Greek word *paschein*, which means to suffer because of one's belief and the practice of those beliefs. Dr. Bryant defines the gift of suffering as "the extraordinary ability to endure hardship, pain, and distress with such an amount of joy and strength to inspire others to endure their suffering and to lead others to accept God's loving redemption made possible in Christ's suffering" (pages 141–42).

Ask for a volunteer to read aloud the definition of suffering on pages 141–42.

Many people do not know how to relate to suffering nor is it something they want. In Christian baptism we acknowledge that we are buried and raised to new life in Christ Jesus. Just as Christ suffered for the redemption of the world, Christians are also called to suffer for others. God's grace enables persons to experience suffering in such a way that it brings honor and glory to God.

Dr. Bryant lists ten statements on page 143. Ask the group to respond to the statements.

Persons with the gift of suffering have a strong sense that there is a higher purpose for their suffering and can often absorb a great deal of pain and suffering of others in Christ's name. They feel deeply the hurts of others and identify with them. They are able to bear the suffering of others because of their strong spirituality and deep spiritual relationship with Christ. They are also aware that suffering was a part of Jesus' life, and he did not complain about his suffering.

Paul wrote about his thorn in the flesh not to complain but as an example of persistence in prayer. Let the group discuss this question: What do you conclude about suffering from the life of Paul?

Dr. Bryant reminds us that suffering is more than a listing of complaints, and the spiritual gift of suffering often rules out talking about the suffering. Sufferers consider it a privilege to suffer with others for Christ's sake. Joy characterizes their spirituality. The quality of religious joy in this gifted person transforms pain and hardship into hope and fulfillment.

Dr. Bryant notes that suffering is not borne solely by poor or oppressed people. He lists examples of gifted leaders who suffer because of their gifts.

❧ How does Dr. Bryant's discussion change your understanding of suffering? When have you witnessed suffering as part of a gift in someone?

Teaching

. . . if it is teaching, let him teach . . . (Romans 12:7).

Gifts enable Christians to serve and build up one another. One way to accomplish this is through teaching. The primary task of the person with this gift is to convey biblical truth to others in a clear and precise way so that the gospel can be grasped and applied to daily life.

Some of the characteristics of this gift are: (1) a thirst for biblical and theological understanding for the word of God, (2) a broad appetite for scriptural correctness, (3) a capacity to study for long periods of time, (4) the ability to make simple the things of God, (5) a joy for reading the Bible, (6) dependence upon the Holy Spirit, and (7) a student orientation. Their teaching is always on a personal and spiritual level with their students.

Teachers use a variety of means and methods to transmit biblical truths. These media may include art, music, painting, drama, and various types of writings.

Paul holds teachers to a high moral and ethical standard. Their teaching must be doctrinally sound and godly and practiced in their daily life (1 Tim. 6:3-5). Teachers are to use their minds to gain godly wisdom so they may correctly impart the word of truth to others. Paul warns those who engage in false teachings which are also harmful to the growth and health of the church. Good teaching is centered in the scriptures and has the potential for producing productive congregations.

❦ List some benefits as well as some potential dangers of this gift?

Voluntary Poverty

For you know the grace of our Lord Jesus Christ, that though he was rich, yet for your sakes he became poor, so that you through his poverty might become rich (2 Corinthians 8:9).

Those endowed with the gift of voluntary poverty live daily with the sufficiency of God's grace. Persons with this gift choose to live a simple and unencumbered life. They do not consider themselves to be poor or dislike material possessions; they prefer to be free of these things so that they can spend more of their time, energies, influence, and spiritual resources to minister.

Whether single or married with family, persons with the gift of voluntary poverty live simplified lifestyles, using their wealth and influence to further the cause of Jesus Christ.

Jesus, Paul, Francis of Assisi, John Wesley, and Mother Teresa are examples of persons with this gift. Their preoccupation is not with the riches of this world but the poverty of those who do not know about the salvation of God. The story about the rich young man suggests that not everyone is willing to accept the gift of voluntary poverty (Mark 10:17-31; Matt. 19:16-30; Luke 18:18-30).

❧ What does Bryant mean when he writes that certain aspects of the gift of poverty apply to all members of the body of Christ?

❧ How is God calling each person to give up some material comfort, including wealth to serve the needs of poor and disadvantaged persons?

❧ What do you feel and think about God's call?

Close this section with silent reflection. Invite the group to respond in silence to these questions.

Wisdom

> *To one there is given through the Spirit the message of wisdom. . . .*
> *(1 Corinthians 12:8)*

Wisdom comes from the Greek word *sophia*, which means a practical application of knowledge (divine or natural) to specific and concrete situations that call on God's favor (grace). These gifted persons have the ability to discern divine and spiritual truths or things of God and to apply them in solving ordinary situations and problems confronting God's people. They strongly believe God's grace applies in solving problems in the everyday routines of life.

They believe God is present and active in God's world and creation. Because of God's active role in creation, God guides and governs all of creation. If we lack wisdom, we need only to ask God for it (James 1:5). God does not desire that anyone lack wisdom. Persons with this gift are open to God's grace to find answers to our questions. Their ability to see into the things of God often leaves others perplexed because of their openness and sensitivity to God.

Read Acts 27 as an example of this gift working in a very practical way to solve a problem.

This is the final gift we will consider in this workbook. We have only scratched the surface of understanding the love and abundant goodness God lavishes upon humanity, both Christians and non-Christians.

Again, ask participants to respond to the main text.

Thanksgiving Prayer (unison)

O God, we give you thanks and praise for your presence, love, and grace through your Spirit. We take delight in you. You are our everything, our all in all. We are grateful to you for sustaining us during this study. We dedicate ourselves to your service as we discover or rediscover our place in the body of Christ. We accept all of the gifts you give to us to manifest your kingdom and to build up the church of Jesus Christ. We are grateful for the new friendships we have developed. We cherish the bond of love that binds us together in Jesus Christ. Help us to build lasting friendships and grant us your grace to work for the good of all humanity in Christ's name. Help us to give continuous service to bring about renewal in our local churches. Amen.

Close this study by asking persons to tell about their experience using this gift. Then read the Thanksgiving Prayer. You may also sing a hymn about the gifts of the Spirit. One beautiful hymn that expresses the variety of God's gifts is "Many Gifts, One Spirit" found in various hymnals.

Practical Applications and Next Steps

Worship

Since beginning this study on the gifts, how have your worship experiences changed? What would you like to see changed within yourself that you feel might change your worship experiences? What would you like to see changed within worship? Name them below.

The Bible

During the next thirty days, read through your workbook giving attention to the entries you made for your reflections and responses. Whenever possible, make cross references to the Bible to reinforce your learning. What is one thing that makes you feel good about having completed this study of the gifts? Share this with one of the members who participated in this study course or someone you have been witnessing to about the gifts.

Prayer

What area of your life still needs God's grace for you to feel free to develop your gifts to help the church grow and mature in Christ? Have you prayed about these? List these areas and work on them one by one until you have the victory for each of them. Ask two other persons to pray for you during this time of spiritual growth. Share with them the progress you are making.

Witnessing

Tell three other persons about what this experience has meant to you and how it is helping you learn how to use your spiritual gifts. Invite them to attend the next workshop on the gifts. Write their names, telephone numbers and addresses in your workbook and the date you talked to them about the study course. Contact them before the next study.

Power

1. In what ways are you limiting God's power from working in your life as a Christian? How do you see the Holy Spirit working within you to change this? List some of the ways you are cooperating with or resisting these changes?

2. What are some signs that your gifts are making a significant difference in the way your local church is opening up more to the gifts of the Spirit?

New Insight

What new understanding have you gained about the gift or gifts you had the most knowledge of? How has this new insight changed the way you practice using the gifts?

Incomplete Data

Which of the gifts not mentioned explicitly in the Bible that were listed in this workbook do you question or struggle with? Explain.

Is It I, Lord?

How has the practice of the spiritual disciplines of prayer, Bible study, worship, and witnessing helped to empower you to use your gifts to serve others better? Now that you have completed this study of the gifts, what is your next step? Where are you going in the ministry and mission of Jesus Christ?

Looking Ahead

For futher enrichment and growth, read through the material in the Appendix.

APPENDIX

Questions Most Frequently Asked About the Gifts

When I travel around the country and hold seminars and workshops or talk to individuals, persons often ask the following questions. My hope is that these answers will stimulate further inquiry and study.

1. Must one be baptized in the Holy Spirit to receive the gifts?

All believers are spiritual persons. A person receives the "gift of the Spirit" at their conversion or spiritual new birth in Christ (1 Cor. 12:3). Paul tells us that every born again person who can say Jesus is Lord has received the Spirit or is baptized in the Spirit. Renewal in the Spirit or the release of the Spirit better describes the work of grace in the life of the believer for now the Spirit has come to endow and empower God's people for works of service in Christ's name.

2. Is speaking in tongues the initial sign of the baptism of the Spirit?

For some persons, speaking in tongues is the initial charismatic experience, but it is not normative. Jesus made it clear that we would know Christians by their love (fulfilling the commandments of loving God, oneself, and one's neighbors). Paul warned that without agape the gifts are of no value (1 Cor. 13). Whether tongues or no tongues, love remains the key to understanding God's will.

3. Does a Christian possess all of the gifts?

I rely on Paul to answer this question. Paul, in 1 Corinthians, stresses the reality that all do not have the same gifts; therefore, no one person can possess all the gifts. Each person receives different gift to serve the body of Christ in a variety of ways so that the needs of other are met.

4. Why don't more people know about the gifts of the Spirit?

Many people are ignorant about the gifts or are not aware that the gifts are available to them. The reason for such widespread ignorance is the lack of teaching about the gifts in the churches. Briefly, these are some other reasons:

Confusion: Some people confuse spiritual gifts with natural talents or the fruit of the Spirit. Others believe that only certain persons receive grace-gifts.

Disobedience: Some people refuse to use their gifts which often leads others to reject the gifts too. Soon people lose interest in the gifts.

Unworthiness: Some people are not open to the gifts because they do not believe they are good enough to receive them. They erroneously associate giftedness with spirituality. They believe that only perfect followers of Jesus qualify to receive the gifts.

Fear: Some do not use or accept the gifts because they fear what others may think of them. They are afraid of failure, that they will not measure up to the expectation of God or others.

Optional: Many believe that the gifts are optional rather than essential and necessary for living a full and meaningful Christian life. They do not understand that without the gifts, the act of worship and service are ineffective and incomplete.

Dispensationalism: Some people believe that God gave gifts at a special period to get the infant church started. Now that the church is established, they think the gifts no longer have value and have been replaced with the written word of God. They deny that they have received any gifts.

5. Why is speaking in tongues so divisive?

People fear tongues because there is a lack of understanding about the nature of the gift. It is through this fear that Satan seeks to distort the value, place, and benefit of tongues. Thus, there is an attempt either to elevate or diminish the gift causing spiritual pride or abuse to limit its value and effectiveness. Confusion also exits about who receives the gift and how and when to use it.

Paul tells us that all the gifts are given for the common good. Rather than causing division in the church, the gifts are given to unify and build up the people of God (Eph. 4:12). Christians receive gifts to help the church grow and mature according to God's will and purpose. When everyone is doing his or her part to build the church, harmony within the church is maintained. Tongues, as God intended them, should not divide the church.

6. Are the gifts relevant for today?

Jesus fully anticipated that the Spirit of God would powerfully and effectively work through all of his followers to continue his mission and ministry. Jesus told his disciples that his followers would achieve even greater works than God had done through him (John 14:12). That is why Jesus asked God to send the promised Holy Spirit upon his followers to empower them with the gift of the Spirit to serve others in his name (Luke 24:49; John 14-16; Acts 1:4-8).

7. Who can receive the gifts of the Spirit?

Only those born of the Spirit can receive the gifts. Persons without the Spirit cannot properly understand, discern, accept or grasp spiritual things because they are foolishness to them (1 Cor. 2:12-16; 12: 3).

8. Why do churches and denominations differ in accepting the gifts?

God gives all of us the gift to make our own choices. Some people exercise their gift of choice not to accept the gifts as a whole or to accept only those gifts that fit their lifestyle, biblical interpretation, or theology. This does not speak ill of anyone, but keeps us aware that God gives many different gifts for the sake of the mission of the church around the world.

9. What happens when people do not use their gifts?

When we do not use our gifts, the church ceases to be the body of Christ (1 Pet. 4:10-11; Eph. 4:12-13). Here are some possibilities:
  a. The church becomes weak and powerless.
  b. Christianity becomes a form of religion without the power.
  c. The people of God become spectators only.
  d. Worship becomes clubby and empty.
  e. The church ceases to be an effective witness to the resurrected life of Jesus Christ.
  f. The creative work and ministries of the Holy Spirit are diminished.

g. Our ability to serve others is limited.

h. The evangelistic ministries of the church are diminished.

10. What happens when we use our gifts?

a. Our Christian faith comes alive.

b. We reveal Christ's love to others.

c. We are empowered to serve others.

d. Others experience God's love, grace, presence, and power through us.

e. Gifts honor and glorify God.

f. The church comes alive through us.

g. The church grows stronger because of us.

11. Do the gifts have less power today than they did in the early church?

The writer of the book of Hebrews tells us that Jesus Christ is the same yesterday and today and forever. Therefore the power of the gifts also remains the same. The gifts of the Spirit always produce the desired results when love is the guiding principle.

12. How can I discover my gift?

Prayerfully seek to discover God's will for your life. Prayer deepens our spiritual relationship with God. Ask the Holy Spirit to reveal the gifts within you. Thank the Holy Spirit for your gifts. Ask the Holy Spirit to help you learn how to use your gifts. Use your gifts for the honor and glory of God. Make the discipline of prayer a part of your spiritual journey. Study the Bible to learn about the gifts. Read and study other resources on the gifts.

Worship allows us to celebrate and give thanks to God for our gifts. People assemble to worship God and to celebrate their rich diversity and unity under the Lordship of Christ. The Holy Spirit uses our gifts to transform worship. The gifts are given to witness to our shared life in Christ.

Sharing your faith in Christ is another way to discover your gifts. The more we use our gifts, the more able we are to use them. The more we serve others, the more gifts we discover within us. God gives us gifts to serve others. When we use our gifts we build up the body of Christ.

Affirmation is another way to discover our gifts. God gives us the ability to discern gifts in others. Every Christian should seek to formulate friendships with mature persons in Christ. Mentoring provides unique opportunities for persons to share questions and insight in spiritual matters that can aid Christian growth and maturity.

A person can also discern gifts by the inner joy that the Spirit produces when the gifts are used in Christ's name. When we discover our gifts, we learn and understand more of God's will for ourselves. When we move in God's grace, we experience the joy of the Lord. Anything we dislike doing or constantly try to get out of is usually a good sign that we might not be gifted for that particular task. When we discover our gift for ministry, it is something we desire to do more than anything. Whatever the gift, the person usually has a passion for it. Not only does it bring us joy, but we also feel that it is a great privilege to share in the mission and ministry of Christ.

A Twelve-Step Self-Evaluation to Discovering Your Gifts

I developed this model as a way to help people discover their grace-gifts. This is a teaching and experiential model. Feel free to use Dr. Bryant's gifts inventory (pages 163–173) to work with this evaluation.

1. Select six of the gifts that interest you from the New Testament or from a gifts list.

2. Select from this list those gifts you have used at least once. If you have not used any of the gifts, select three of the gifts you have a strong interest in.

3. List those gifts you have used two or three times.

4. List those gifts you have used four or more times.

5. Which of the gifts have you done the most reading or research about?

6. Place all of the gifts into two groups. In one group, place the gifts you have studied, used, or have a strong interest in. Place the remaining gifts into the second group.

7. Which of the gifts in the first group give you the most joy or fulfillment?

8. Which of the gifts in the first group has someone else affirmed in you?

9. If you had to give up any one of the gifts, which one would you miss the most?

10. Find another person who is also seeking to discover his or her gifts. Become prayer partners for each other to remain focused and encouraged.

11. Which of the gifts do you believe the Holy Spirit has gifted you with? Did this evaluation confirm any of the gifts the Holy Spirit had given to you?

12. Disclose to your prayer partner what you have discovered about your grace-gifts. Praise God for the gifts God has given you, and ask the Holy Spirit for wisdom and guidance in using them. Remember this passage of scripture as you continue your study of your grace-gifts. "I am confident of this, that the one who began a good work among you will bring it to completion by the day of Jesus Christ" (Phil. 1:6, NSRV).

STUDY EXERCISE

Now that you have completed the twelve-step exercise, what gifts did you discover? The following exercise will help you to think more seriously about these gifts.

1. List, in the margin, your discovered gifts according to your first, second, and third choices.

2. For the next several days, spend time in prayer concerning your potential gifts. Ask the Lord to help you determine which gifts are God's desire for you. ·

3. During the next month or two, try to learn all you can about the gifts named in your first group. Use a variety of resources, including the Bible, books, periodicals, and magazines.

4. Experiment with using your gifts whenever the opportunity presents itself.

5. Keep a journal to note the place, situation, how you have been called to use your gifts, the effectiveness, and the results of using your gifts. Make notes concerning your failures and problems in using the gifts. Learning from failures remains a very important way to grow.

6. When possible, observe the way others use the same gifts. Learn firsthand from them how to use the gifts and how not to use them.

7. Try to discern your true gifts. Usually, the gifts that produce the greatest joy within you, or give you the greatest expression of sharing in the ministry of Christ, are your true gifts.

8. List the other gifts that you think complement your gifts. If these gifts were not a part of the gifts in your first or second group, do a study of them also.

9. Experiment with using these new gifts. Which of these new gifts interest you the most and the least? Put the gift that interests you the least in your second group.

10. Select one or two of the gifts from your second group to experiment with. From this group, select the gifts that interest you the most, then follow the twelve steps with this gift(s).

11. Clarify your own ideas about your gifts and determine how best to use your gifts.

12. Remember these five points about the gifts: (1) God designed, (2) God inspired, (3) God revealed, (4) God given, and (5) God energized.

13. Remember: The gifts are given to be used for the common good of all. We are to use our gifts according to the faith we have been given. Without love, our gifts are both empty and ineffective.
Thank God for your gifts and use your gifts for the praise and glory of God, in the Spirit of Christ, and in the power of the Holy Spirit.

WHAT ARE YOUR NEXT STEPS?

What do you intend to do next? How do you plan to use your gifts in your local church? What do you expect from your church? Write down your plans and share them with your pastor in order to get a response. Work within the structure of your particular local church. Do everything with love and in the Spirit of Christ, for the glory of God, and in the power of the Holy Spirit. God bless your ministry!

About the Author

The Reverend John I. Penn is the Director of Spiritual Formation and Healing at The Upper Room in Nashville, Tennessee. As an ordained minister in The United Methodist Church, he has served pastorates in the Peninsula-Delaware Conference. He also taught high school for more than twenty years.

The author, a native of Roanoke, Virginia, has written booklets on healing and on the gifts of the Holy Spirit. He holds degrees from the University of Arkansas at Pine Bluff (Bachelor of Science in Music Education), Oral Robert's University (Master in Theology), and Drew Seminary and Eastern Baptist Theological Seminaries (Master of Divinity).

Rev. Penn enjoys playing tennis, writing, composing music, and reading. He is married to Gloria, and they have six children and four grandchildren.